THE BITTER END

Paul Colby during the Bitter End press party for the feature-length documentary of Ramblin' Jack Elliott, *The Ballad of Ramblin' Jack*. Originally shot for *Vanity Fair*. *Courtesy of Annie Leibovitz.*

THE BITTER END

Hanging Out at America's Nightclub

Paul Colby

with Martin Fitzpatrick

Foreword by Kris Kristofferson

Cooper Square Press

First Cooper Square Press edition 2002

This Cooper Square Press hardcover edition of *The Bitter End* is an original publication. It is published by arrangement with the authors.

Published by Cooper Square Press
A member of the Rowman & Littlefield Publishing Group
200 Park Avenue South, Suite 1109
New York, NY 10003
www.coopersquarepress.com

Distributed by National Book Network

Library of Congress Cataloging-in-Publication Data
Colby, Paul, 1917–
    The Bitter End: hanging out at America's nightclub / by Paul Colby with Martin Fitzpatrick.
        p. cm.
Includes index.
    ISBN 0-8154-1206-1 (cloth : alk. paper)
    1. Colby, Paul, 1917–   2. Impresarios—United States—Biography.   3.
Bitter End (Nightclub)   I. Fitzpatrick, Martin, 1952–   II. Title.
    ML429.C567 A3 2002
        791'.092—dc21

                                        2002003977

⊖ ™
    The paper used in this publication meets the minimum requirements of American National Standard for Information Sciences—Permanence of Paper for Printed Library Materials, ANSI/NISO Z39.48–1992.
Manufactured in the United States of America.

For Pamela Ann Wilson
for standing by me,
and for Fred Weintraub and
Joel Selvin, without whom
this book would never have happened.
P. C.

For Kate and for Paul,
who made it all happen.
M. F.

Contents

ACKNOWLEDGMENTS

THE AUTHORS WOULD like to thank the following people for their generous help and fond remembrances while we wrote this book: Al Alvino, Sid Bernstein, Theo Bikel, Oscar Brand, David Brenner, Marshall Brickman, Charlie Brown, Hamilton Camp, Richard Campbell, Dick Cavett, Len Chandler, Tom Chapin, Jim Dawson, Bill Deseta, Art D'Lugoff, Weston Gavin, Jon Gibbs, Kenny Gorka, Wavy Gravy, Laura Harris, Judy Henske, Jake Holmes, Janis Ian, Tommy James, Robert Klein, Steve Landesberg, Harold Leventhal, Lenny Levine, Buzzy Linhart, Rick Maher, Len Maxwell, Curtis Mayfield, Tracy Newman, Tom Paxton, Sharon and Kate Petronaci, Dick Reicheg, Paul Rizzo, Harry Robinson, Jack and Jane Rollins, Manny Roth, Tracy Ryan, Bill Saluga, Vin Scelsa, John Sebastian, Tom Senif, Brian Sennet, Richmond Shepard, Dave Van Ronk, Eric Weissberg, David Wilkes, Bill Withers, and Peter Yarrow.

Kris Kristofferson and Paul Colby in the seventies.

*F*OREWORD

I FIRST HEARD of the Bitter End in the early sixties when I was in the army doing a three-year tour in Germany. I was playing in a band during my off time and dreaming of making music for a living. Our Dobro player, a West Pointer and the only real musician among us, gave me a Peter, Paul and Mary album to learn a couple of songs by. The best tunes were written by this new kid who was old-timer classic and original at the same time named Bob Dylan. Everything about that album burned its way into my brain—not only the songs like "Blowin' in the Wind" but also the look of the red brick wall of the Bitter End where the album cover was shot.

The place was something of a shrine by the time I finally came to Greenwich Village, a lifetime later, at the end of the sixties. That's when Shel Silverstein introduced me to Paul Colby and the Bitter End and all the other wonderful bars and clubs on Bleecker and MacDougal Streets that seemed to be full of artists, poets, dreamers, and drunks. Like the Ryman Auditorium back home in Nashville, the Bitter End was the Mother Church, run by a guy whose heart was into it and for whom what happened on stage was all that mattered. The Bitter End was designed to focus attention on the artist, and the audiences listened and were hip and responded because they were full of people like Bobby Neuwirth, Larry Poons, Andy Warhol, Patti Smith, Ramblin' Jack Elliott, Odetta, and always the possibility of Dylan. That was my world. It was a magical place at a magical time, and I was hungry but happy and creative. And Paul Colby had the best seat in the house.

Fortunately for those who worked for him, Paul was on the side of the angels. (Which is to say he was on our side; he loves artists and fights fiercely for them.) It was an atmosphere where everything was possible and some special moments got made. Like the night Paul let me put a couple of guys nobody outside of Chicago had ever heard of on my show. It all started when Paul Anka introduced himself to me on a flight into Chicago. He told me he was working the Fairmont and was going to perform one of my songs at his gig. I was doing a week at a little club called the Quiet Night, and we said we would try to get together. My schedule (and my attire) prevented me from going to the Fairmont, so Paul Anka stopped by the Quiet Night, where I was sharing the bill with Steve Goodman. Steve knocked us out with his songs like "City of New Orleans" and "Sam Stone" written by a friend of his whom he wanted us to meet. I was sick and road-weary from travel and three shows a night for the last eighteen months, but Steve was insistent. So we all went over to another club called the Earl of Old Town to meet John Prine. The club was closed and dark by the time we got there, chairs on the table, and John and his wife waiting for us, asleep in a booth. I couldn't believe the poor guy was going to wake up to sing for strangers, but he stepped up to the mike and proceeded to sing one absolute killer after another: "Paradise," "Donald and Lydia," "Hello in There." He sang a dozen or so, and when he was finished, we made him start over. I remember thinking it was like stumbling onto Dylan for the first time.

Later, when we were all celebrating up in Paul Anka's penthouse suite, Paul said to them, "Would you consider letting me fly you to New York to discuss publishing and recording?" Steve said, "Would you like to see a short, fat Jewish kid dive in a bowl of chicken soup?"

I said I was going to be working at the Bitter End and if they could come by, I'd put them on stage. I told them the owner was a good man, that he dug music and musicians and would help us. Well, of course, he is and he did . . . but there are realities, and Steve and John only had time to do a couple of songs during my first set. They were so great that Paul Colby came up during the break and said, "Listen, you put those guys onstage again and let them sing as long as they want to." Our friend Jerry Wexler was in the audience. He sent his wife home in the limo and came back for a night of real music, after which he signed John to Atlantic Records and Paul Anka put Steve on the Buddha label.

Not all episodes ended so magically. Once, between shows, I was told there was a guy outside waiting in line and causing trouble. He was insisting that he speak to me. Before they called the police, I went outside and was confronted by a young guy in a dirty field jacket. He had long, sweaty blond hair, and he looked like he had been standing too close to the flame. He nailed me with blazing eyes and said, "You're my fifth favorite songwriter!" Dead serious, I said, "Who are your first four?" I think he said Dylan, Leonard Cohen, Phil Ochs, and Neil Young. "Let him in," I said, and Paul let him in and sat him in the first row, where he proceeded to fall asleep and snore so loudly that the audience rose up in anger and threw him out.

I'll always be grateful for the time I spent at the Bitter End working or just hanging out. If anything, the house looks holier in my heart, colored by all the love and laughter and lifting of spirits that went on in there. On behalf of all of us in the business of moving the emotions with our imagination, special thanks to Paul Colby for being one of us.

KRIS KRISTOFFERSON
Malibu, California
March 2002

PREFACE

WHENEVER ANYONE ASKS us what this book is about, we usually say, "It's about you." We do not mean to be sappy or sentimental. Anyone who lived through the sixties will know what we are talking about. There is always a strong connection between artist and audience, and never so much as in the sixties. Most of the artists who came of age in the sixties have tried to maintain that feeling. The music and comedy of that era informed our politics, social behavior, morals, and love life. It helped us decide what we were going to teach our children and how we would conduct our lives. Never before had music played such an integral part in the politics and manners of our country. Not since Jonathan Swift had humor been so stinging, scathing, and devastatingly honest.

Today we live in an age of virtual reality; the sixties may have been the last time when artist and audience connected by physically touching each other. We fought our causes on the streets together, marched together, sang together, smoked together, lived and loved together. The artists were literally ten feet away. Much of that pattern has changed, with one notable exception: the Bitter End. We still do it the old-fashioned way.

This book is not a tell-all book. Most of the period we discuss is the sixties, so if it makes you feel good, you may assume that practically everyone mentioned in this book slept with practically everyone else at one time or another. Nor is it a book about everyone's personal moments of self-destruction. Practically everyone in this book took a ride on that roller coaster at one time or another, and most got off in time. This is essentially a celebration—a celebration of a magnificent flowering of musical and comedic art that no one has seen the like of since. For those of you who lived through it, we hope this book will bring back good memories. For those of you who were too young or not around yet, we hope it will show you what show business was like and what it could be again.

PAUL COLBY
MARTIN FITZPATRICK

1

SWEET BEGINNINGS

Paul Colby: artist, award-winning furniture maker, tremendous purveyor of talent, raconteur, businessman extraordinaire, and the only guy I know who ever swiped a nightclub.

—**Robert Klein,** in conversation

"YOU'RE FIRED!"

That's how it all began. For about nine years I managed the premier coffeehouse in Greenwich Village, the Bitter End. But in 1974 the owner, Fred Weintraub, fired me. Here's what happened.

The Bitter End had been in business since 1961. Virtually everybody in the entertainment business got their start there or played there until they hit the big time. I mean everybody. I'll come to all that later. By 1974, I realized that the coffeehouse days were over. The entertainment world was going through another one of its periodic convulsions. The public's longing for quiet, introspective nights with hip comics and soul-searching folksingers was fading. The kids who had hung out during the sixties had aged and become adults in spite of themselves. And the following generation of audiences was not so innocent. People wanted to be able to drink, and the Bitter End didn't have a liquor license.

The Bitter End is located at 147 Bleecker Street, in the heart of Greenwich Village. Next door was a little gin joint called the Now Bar, which catered to all the workingmen who were busy building the new New York University library just around the corner. When the library was finished, so was the Now Bar.

I tried talking Fred into buying the bar. The only other business the Now Bar had was when Bob Dylan or Kris Kristofferson and I, or any of the other acts that played the club, came in for a quick one. A lot of Bitter End customers came in too. Buying the Now Bar seemed like a natural. Fred wasn't around much by 1974. He was out in California trying to become a Hollywood producer, wheeling and dealing with film moguls. He wasn't interested. So I bought the place myself.

When Fred found out, he was pretty mad. He thought I should be concentrating all my efforts on the Bitter End, which indeed I was. He didn't want competition. But the Now Bar was only next door, and it didn't offer entertainment, just food and drink. In my new enterprise, I had two experienced partners to help me out, and it didn't take a lot of effort to keep a good eye on both places.

One day I got a call at the Now Bar. It was Fred. "What are you doing there?" he said. "Fred, I just stopped in for a minute. The Bitter End is running smoothly, like it always has been." But he wouldn't let it go. "Fred, if I open up a dry-cleaning store in the Bronx with my brother, do I have to ask your permission?" He didn't like that at all.

That's when he fired me.

Without sounding egotistical, I was the best manager the Bitter End ever had. Everybody in the neighborhood was shocked because it was well known that until I came on the scene, Fred had had a tough time keeping managers. One person in particular, the landlord, who didn't like Fred, was very upset. Fred and the landlord had had a tangle over a commercial lease for a restaurant, the Tin Angel, that we ran back in the sixties. Joni Mitchell titled one of her first songs in memory of it. Fred backed out of the lease when business fell off, and the landlord was pretty sore, but there was nothing he could do about it.

Resigned, I concentrated on the Now Bar, while Fred brought in a woman from his management company, Fredanna, to run the club. She was a pleasant woman who booked acts for the Bitter End's college circuit, but managing a prestigious club was beyond her. I think she must have realized as much when the bookings that I had previously arranged finally ran out. It was early in the summer of 1974. She went out and hired a single cockamamie band, ironically called Fred, booked them for the entire summer, and went off to Europe for a vacation. The band's manager was given the keys to the place and was expected to pay the rent. Fred the band turned out to be not very good. It was a bad draw even in the dog days of summer. After covering the rent, they barely had enough money left over for cigarettes.

One day the landlord came into my new place for a beer. Maybe we had two or three, but the landlord made me a proposition I couldn't refuse. We told the manager of the band not to pay the rent. That way he and his boys could at least eat. When they didn't pay the rent for a couple of months, the landlord put a seal on the door and closed the place up. When the new manager returned from Europe, she found a padlock on the door and called Fred out in California. Fred was too busy trying to jump-

3

start his ninth or tenth career and conceded defeat.

I got the lease to both places, cut a hole in the wall to connect the businesses, and opened up later that year as the Other End. About six years later the Bitter End name became available again, and I grabbed it and rechristened the club. We are now at the beginning of a new century and the Bitter End is still going strong. Fred stopped in a few years after I got the place and congratulated me. He was happy out in California and apparently didn't mind me outwitting him. We are still friends to this day.

This is the story of my life and, by extension, a history of the most famous nightclub in the world, the Bitter End.

MY NAME IS PAUL COLBY, and I was born in Philadelphia the year George M. Cohan's "Over There" and W. C. Handy's "Beale Street Blues" were written and being sung at every parade and bar in America. Five years later, my family moved to New York City. My father was a tailor, and he set up his home and business on the Lower East Side. I had three brothers. I grew up during the lean years of the Great Depression and watched my father work his ass off. I won't go into any of the sad stories—very little food, no heat, four in a bed—except to say that it was all true. My folks were Jewish but not very religious. My father believed in the Golden Rule, which is what I like to think of as his legacy to me.

I went to high school and took some courses, but I floundered. One of my teachers said, "You're too creative for this kind of thing. You have to get out of here." So, they sent me to Textile High School, which doesn't exist anymore. It was on Eighteenth Street. At Textile, I was able to express my creative side. I worked hard and finally graduated. After school I did my service in the military and then looked for work, a job, anything. But I had no experience. I couldn't break through.

I took odd jobs cleaning up offices in Manhattan. I became a shipping clerk in a novelty house on Broadway and Eighteenth Street. I remember working there for quite a while. Then I ran into a friend of mine who I grew up with in the Bronx. His name was Harold Leventhal. Harold was working for Irving Berlin Publishing Company. "Why don't you come out with me one night and I'll show you what I do," said Harold. "You know, hang out." So, I took Harold up on his offer and hung out with him one night. It was a gas. Harold would take songs, sheet music, to any of the bands that were playing in New York. It was one of the ways a song got out to the public back then. Forget about MTV. This was before disc jockeys. Songs had to be played by live musicians at live locations. Mostly it was journeymen players, local sidemen, people not particularly distinguished. But with any luck, you might get your song played by the best in the business. At that time, that meant Benny Goodman or the Dorsey brothers. They had what they called location shots. Harold went around plugging the songs he represented for his publishing firm. This was in the early 1940s.

I told Harold, "This is nice. You get dressed up, you go out, you buy a drink and the company pays for it. And all you do is try and peddle your songs. How do you get into this business?" I went out with him a couple of more times. I started meeting people who mattered, and I decided this is what I wanted to do.

I became a counterboy. People would call up and ask for copies of songs, and I delivered them to the radio stations. I was basically a glorified errand boy, but I didn't care. I loved it. You had to get dressed up, you had to have your nails manicured, and you had to look like one of the big boys in the business.

Over the next few years, I worked for the Warner Brothers publishing empire. I put music into the hands of a lot of bands at places like the New Yorker, the Waldorf Astoria, the Rainbow Room, and Jack Dempsey's.

The songs would then go out over the wire. The more the bands played the songs, the more they got requested and put on "the sheet," which was a chart much like *Billboard* magazine does today with their top one hundred. Eventually I started getting songs on the air, and people took notice. I became a song plugger.

A song plugger was an official. I had to be in the union and pay dues. I found the whole process fascinating, and I got good at it. Eventually I went to work for Regent Music, which was owned by Benny Goodman and his brothers, Harry and Gene. Because he didn't play in the band anymore, Harry actually ran the business. I worked closely with Harry, and we got to be good friends. Regent Music published all the swing songs that Benny did, and through that, I got to meet and know Benny, Louis Armstrong, and my favorite, Duke Ellington. One day an emissary of Duke's came by and asked for a favor. Duke's son, Mercer, was draft age, and Duke wanted to keep him from going overseas. I knew a guy from my army days who knew a general, and I made the necessary calls. Mercer wound up working for the U.S. Army Band. Duke wanted it kept private, and I honored his wishes. Mercer didn't have a clue and still doesn't to this day. I did it as a favor for Duke. There were lots of people who had money and influence who were doing the same thing and continue to do it today. Just look at most of our modern politicians. I never did like double standards. After I arranged everything, Duke wanted to formally meet me. He was grateful for my help and my discretion. From that day on, every time he was in New York, I was backstage, hanging out with Duke Ellington.

Then I got an opportunity to work for Barton Music. Barton Music was owned by a guy named Benny Barton, a money-man named Hank Sanicola, and a singer named Frank Sinatra. When the moment came, I grabbed for it. To this day, I don't know why Frank and Hank ever went into business with Benny Barton. Barton was a dapper dresser, articulate, but not very savvy or aggressive. He was a small-time publisher, and I guess they figured they could use him. Later on, Benny got his daughter, Eileen, a recording contract. She actually landed a top-ten hit in 1956 with a song called "If I Knew You Were Coming I'd'a Baked a Cake." Benny wasn't a good manager, and that was the first and last hit she had. But this was 1946, and all of us were about to take a big step up the ladder.

I started out performing the kind of duties you would expect a song plugger to undertake. At that time we had our first big hit, "Saturday Night Is the Loneliest Night in the Week," and there was a lot of excitement in the air. That record catapulted Frank right over the top. Then we had one hit song after another. "There's No You," "If You Are But a Dream," "Full Moon and Empty Arms." I was busy as hell, but slowly my duties basically became hanging out with Sinatra. Frank was separated from his first wife, Nancy, and on his own at that time. I was backstage most nights, and I'll never forget it.

I especially remember helping backstage at the Paramount in that mob of kids. I was young, too, after all. It was a shock to me because I had never been involved in anything like this before. This was a real happening. Maybe one of the first. Maybe our grandmothers went crazy like that for Caruso, I don't know. I remember a girl coming up to me and saying, "I'll do anything you want if you get me a ticket to one of the shows." I walked away rapidly. I thought, "Holy shit! Am I supposed to take advantage of this?" It was more glamorous and decadent than anything I had ever known. Looking back on it now, I must say that it was very good experience for me and helped me prepare for and understand the sixties more than I might have.

Sinatra got to like me and depend on me. He would call the office almost every day and say, "Paul, come on over." Although he was making a lot of his now classic recordings, in a certain sense these were lean years for Sinatra. He had his troubles. Plenty of people were down on him for leaving Nancy, and his inner circle was small. He was staying at the Hampshire House, and some days we would hang out all morning.

I'd leave the office, stop by Horn and Hardart's and pick up coconut Danish, and we'd have coffee. We had a great time talking and hanging out. One day Benny Barton said, "Where are you going?" I said, "I'm going to the Hampshire House to see Frank." Benny said, "No, you're not. You don't work for Frank Sinatra. You work for Barton Music." I remember looking at Benny and saying very distinctly, "Well, call Frank and tell him I'm not coming." There was a pause and Benny said, "Go ahead." Even back then you just didn't talk to Frank that way.

I believe very strongly that this was one of the reasons why I was eventually fired from Barton Music. I found myself being Frank's right-hand man. Benny Barton objected to that. Of course, in the entertainment business, I don't care whether you're a star musician or actor or just a song plugger, you're always in between jobs. I began to enjoy the moment, and I never enjoyed it so much as when I hung out with Frank. I was constantly going to the airport to pick up Ava Gardner. Many times, I was her "date" if Frank couldn't make it or had something else going on. One night I took her to the ballet with Van Heflin and his wife. It seemed I was always taking people out or picking people up at Frank's request. We often went shopping together, and he began to confide in me. Once at the Hampshire House he was very upset because he had had a terrific fight with an old lady on a flight back to New York. She was giving him a hard time because she claimed he should have been in the army instead of singing songs. Of course, he regretted yelling at her and began to seriously question his motives. I found him very intellectual.

Frank was a giver. I always resented it when people wrote bad things about him. He took me out to dinner, bought me watches, clothing, mementos. There was no reason to do this other than thoughtfulness. He was the kind of guy who would give you the shirt off his back. In fact, he did many times. I had so many shirts from Sinatra that I used to cut out the "FS" on the pockets, put it in a frame, and give it to a girl. It actually helped in some of my romances. If I cut two inches off the trousers, I could wear his suits too. If I didn't look quite sharp enough, he would pick out a suit jacket for me, people would be sent for, and my pants would be pressed, shoes shined, even though I was only going to the airport to pick up Ava or some other starlet.

One night the phone rang. It was Frank. "Paul, what are you doing Friday night?" I said, "Nothing at all." He said, "That's what you think. You're taking a couple of girls out and bringing them to the Copa," where he was appearing at the time. When I picked the girls up, I discovered that there were six of them. And they were all blind! He didn't tell me how many or that they were blind, but that was Frank. What did I care? I had six beautiful girls on my arm, front-row seats at the Copacabana, and I was the host. I'll never forget listening to Frank sing while I danced with them one by one, guiding them around the floor and telling them exactly what the place looked like, the colors, the lights, the palm trees. And it was all on Frank. It was the kind of thing he did all the time.

I became quite acclimated to Frank's demands and procedures, especially the backstage routine. And I must admit to something, which was not particularly nice but was part of the job. There were always two or three dozen photos of Frank that I would have to sign. I would say that there are quite a few photographs of Sinatra out there that I actually signed.

I had a great time when he finally married Ava. He took two suites at the Drake Hotel and broke through the wall, making one luxurious apartment. He had a live-in Chinese cook, and I had the key to the apartment. Frank and Ava weren't there all the time, and the Chinese cook wanted to cook for somebody, so he cooked for me. I used to bring a girl up there occasionally. Of course, I always left the place neat.

It was just as amazing to be around Ava as it was to be around Frank. She was beautiful beyond your wildest imagination. One day Frank asked me to stop by the apartment and give something to Ava. A gift, a message, I don't remember. I knocked on the door, the door opened, and there was Ava, stark naked. Maybe she thought I was Frank, I have no idea. She said, "Oh," quite innocently, and then, "I'll be right back." She turned and ran down the hall without closing the door, and I, being the cad that I am, watched her disappear into one of the rooms. She got into a robe and came back and took whatever I had to give her or tell her. She never referred to it. She didn't get angry or sprinkle me with water and turn me into a deer like Athena. I don't know why she didn't close the door, but it was to my advantage. I became one of the few people who saw Ava Gardner naked.

It was apparent that I wasn't the most liked guy around Barton Music, but when I wasn't with Frank, I did my job well. Frank was traveling more and more, but he was still a presence. Once I got this fabulously expensive phone bill, around three thousand dollars. I went to Benny Barton and said, "What the hell is this?" "Don't worry," he said, "Just give me the bill." I finally coaxed it out of him. The telephone operators would sell Frank's number to the fan clubs, so Frank and Ava would have to keep switching phone numbers, and someone had had Frank use mine for a couple of months. I got the bill, but he took care of it.

I lived in the Village at that time on Eighth Street, and I got a phone call from a British operator one night that threw me off. It was early Sunday morning. I was asleep, I know that. "Is there a Mr. Paul Colby there?" in this heavy English accent. "This is he," I said. I was impressed. "I have Mr. Frank Sinatra on the line." Frank gets on the phone and says, "Paul, do me a favor. I want you to go out and pick me up a thousand powder puffs." "Frank," I said casually, "I don't want to be nosy, but what the hell do you need a thousand powder puffs for?" And he told me the chorus girls in London had a shortage of powder puffs. He told me a pilot from Pan Am named Bob would come by my house and pick them up. And he did.

The next week I got another call. Ava had gone to London to join him. "Paul?" "Yes, Frank." "I want you to pick me up a side of ham, a quart of half-and-half, some butter, eggs"— I can't remember the whole menu. "It's a pain in the ass trying to find this stuff over here. Bob will pick it up." I went out and bought the food, and good old Bob came by and picked it up. He was flying to London that night.

I should have seen it coming and talked to Frank about it, but by then he had pretty much relocated to Beverly Hills and was concentrating on keeping up with Ava. Benny hired a guy named Charlie Ross, who was a professional music guy, very suave, man of the world, who started to take charge, and sure enough, I was fired. Nobody in the main office protested, and Frank was more or less cutting his ties. I was being paid back for being friendly to Frank. To be honest, without Frank around, the job wasn't worth it anyway. This was around 1950, and I decided I would try my hand out West.

I eased my way out of New York with no real plan in mind. I made a stop-off in Chicago with another firm called London Music, which was owned by Guy Lombardo. Either Guy Lombardo wasn't my cup of tea or Chicago was too cold, I can't remember, but I left after about a year and finally got to California. I looked up an old friend named Pete Kameron. He was another Bronx boy who had gravitated toward the music business. Pete's character had not quite formed into utter ruthlessness at that time. In fact, we were actually friendly. Unfortunately, or fortunately, I could never establish myself out in California. Frank was traveling all over the world by then, and I was never able to meet him again. I kept meaning to look him up, but time and circumstances, fate even, seemed to be against it. The only interesting thing that happened to me in California involved Peggy Lee.

One day Pete Kameron and I went to hang out with Juggy Gayles. I knew Juggy when he worked for Irving Berlin Publishing as a song plugger. Juggy did work for Sinatra and was most famous for getting Irving Berlin's "White Christmas" on the air. Juggy invited us down to a recording studio where Peggy Lee was working. She was covering "Fever" by Leiber and Stoller, a song originally recorded by Little Willie Littlefield. The producers felt that the song didn't sound right in the chorus. They wanted more voice. "Hey, you guys. Get in here." One of the producers stuck the three of us in a booth and we sang back-up vocals on Peggy's record, which became a monster hit. Juggy Gayles worked in the music business until he died at eighty-six years old. Even though he is associated with Tin Pan Alley, he remained contemporary. His last venture involved a partnership with Sleeping Bag Records, which produced hip-hop.

California turned out not to be my cup of tea either. Whatever job I had, I lost it. I was broke. I stayed with Pete for a while but began to yearn for New York. To me, that's where the music business was and always will be. Like Woody Allen, I'm an unrepentant Gotham chauvinist.

I told Pete I had to get back to New York, and he said, "Do you want to work your way back? I need a road manager for an all-girl, colored jazz band." The only thing I had to my name was a 1942 Lincoln Zephyr, which was just the kind of car you need for a long and crowded haul. Times being what they were, I accepted the job.

When I met the band, I discovered there were actually three black girls and two white girls. Two of the original black girls had dropped out. This caused us some absurd logistical problems because the tour took us all through the Southland where segregation was the law! The two white girls actually had to wear blackface in order to perform. And it couldn't look fake. If we played in black venues, it didn't seem to matter that much, but most of our gigs were in white establishments with either "no colored allowed" or the black clientele sitting way in the rear or up in the balcony. The point was that there was no mixing of the races whatsoever.

One night we played a gig in Hattiesburg, Mississippi. There was a portly sheriff watching the show and looking very closely at the stage. He wore his gun, of course, and the club owner was a nervous wreck. "Don't fuck with him," he whispered to me. "He's got three notches in his belt." Of course I said something mildly sarcastic, and the sheriff said, "Yaova heya sayacajun?" I said, "What did you say?" The sheriff said again, "Yaova heya sayacajun?" I couldn't understand one word. The black barman translated. "He said, 'Did you ever hear of segregation?'" His trigger finger was itchy, that's for sure. That sheriff knew there was something wrong with our band, but he couldn't put his stubby finger on it.

In New Orleans, we didn't get away with it. I was sick that night and couldn't go to the gig, so Pete went. About two hours later, Pete ran up to my room and said, "Get the car. We're leaving." Somebody figured out that two of the black girls weren't really black. Whatever taboo was in place, we had somehow shattered it to smithereens. We had to leave in our socks.

In Dallas we were pulled over by a cop who was so proud and so fat he was ready to burst. "Ah bin followin' you fuh miles, an' ah finally gotcha." "Got me for what?" I said. "Eighteen miles in a fifteen-mile zone." I wanted to kill him. Pete said, "Will you shut up? We're not in New York." We had to go right to the town hall and pay the ticket.

At a service station in Arkansas, we stopped to get gas and water. The owner came out and said, "Please, please get your gas and get out." They didn't want to be seen with black people in that gas station. I think if they ever found out I was Jewish to boot, that would have pushed them over the edge. During the day when the white girls didn't have to be in makeup, I took pictures in front of the hotels that said "No Colored Allowed" so they could send them home to their folks.

There was a big club on the border between Texas and Oklahoma. You could buy the whiskey in Oklahoma, but you couldn't drink it. You had to take it back to Texas to drink it, but it was all in the same place. It was nuts. There were signs that said "This Side to Buy" and "This Side to Drink." In the South at that time, there was a different law for everything every fifteen feet. At some point I said, "Pete, I'm leaving." I couldn't take it anymore.

I finally got back to New York. I was seeing a girl named Jean, whom I later married. I was living off and on with Jean during the time I was working with Sinatra. She objected to my night work for Sinatra because it was taking me away from her, but after much haranguing and separation, we finally came to some kind of conclusion. Anyway, we got married. About ten years later, we reached a different conclusion and got divorced. But for those ten years or so, I left the music business and tried to make a business out of a hobby I had, which was building furniture.

When I lived in California for that short time, I had access to a garage and tools. I reacquainted myself with the skills I had developed at Textile High School and got very handy and began making furniture for my friends. I enjoyed working with my hands, and people seemed to be satisfied with my stuff. When I got back to New York, word had spread. I remember the president of Decca Records, Morty Palitz, and his wife, Chickie, who was an interior designer, asked me to make them a coffee table. At first, I turned her down, but when I found out it was for Duke Ellington's house, I made the table. It didn't take long until Cy Coleman was calling me to make cabinet pieces and other furniture. Jean and I set up shop as Colby Associates. It took about a year or two to get established, but I became a sort of furniture maker to the stars. I made furniture not only for Duke and Cy but also for Tony Bennett, Morris Levy, Diahann Carroll, even Miles Davis. Miles and I got to be good friends.

While Miles was making good money, he was also pissing a lot of it away. One day after delivering some end tables for him, I said, "Miles, why don't you buy yourself a nice brownstone, fix up the bottom floor for yourself, and rent out the top floors? Then you'll have a nice place to live plus money coming in." Miles did what Miles always did. He mumbled something you couldn't understand but otherwise kept quiet. About a month later, he was moving my furniture into his own brownstone. It was one of the best business moves he ever made.

Anyway, my furniture sold. It got reviewed in the *New York Times* and *House Beautiful* and was anthologized as an example of the best of contemporary design. But eventually I overextended myself, ran into debt, ended my marriage, and started working in apartment buildings installing and fixing elevators. It was the 1960s, and I was at a dead end. I needed to get back into the music business. But the world had changed, especially the music world. There wasn't one dominant musical form anymore like there was before the war. Big-band and club singers could still make a living, but there were other genres, like rock and roll, forcing their way into the market. All you had to do was look at a jukebox. For years, the style of music was big band and singers performing standards. Then suddenly Little Richard and Elvis were rubbing shoulders with Rosemary Clooney and Perry Como. Folk music was starting to become a big draw. The more offbeat a performer you were, the more the public seemed to search you out. Radio deejays like Alan Freed were making headlines. Who needed a song plugger anymore? I was still hanging out uptown, but all the action seemed to be coming from Greenwich Village.

Around 1965 a pop singer and friend of mine, Billy Fields, was involved in a small coffeehouse in the Village called the Bitter End. The owner had a management company, and Billy was running acts like Neil Diamond and the Four Seasons. The owner was going through managers like Kleenex during flu season, and he wanted someone stable to help run the place. "It's the hottest little club in the world, and all they serve is ice-cream sodas." I went down with Billy one night and caught some of the acts. He told me we should meet on the corner of Bleecker and Sullivan Streets. "I think tonight it's Simon and Garfunkel," he said in a distracted manner. I misunderstood him. I thought we were supposed to meet at Simon and Garfunkel. I thought Simon and Garfunkel was a drugstore.

I went and saw the show. I liked the place. I had no idea what I could do, but I wanted to do something. I liked the Village, and I recognized some people hanging out there. My old friend Harold Leventhal was hanging out. He was managing Pete Seeger and trying to get Woody Guthrie's kid Arlo started in the business. Jack Rollins and Charlie Joffe were always around working new prospects. I met my old friend Sid Bernstein, who brought the Beatles to America and helped fuel the British Invasion. Sid would bring his kids down to the club and listen to the hootenannies. A lot of the business seemed to be handled out on the sidewalk in front of the club with the agents, managers, and artists sitting on the trunks and hoods of cars. There was an easygoing swagger to the whole thing that I loved. And it was nice to be back in the Village. It seemed that everybody who was hip, and a lot of people who wanted to look hip, were hanging out below Fourteenth Street. It didn't take me long to realize that, from my end of the business, Greenwich Village was the place to be.

2

THE GREENWICH VILLAGE RENAISSANCE

If you knew where you were or what you were doing in the sixties, you probably weren't there.

—**Wavy Gravy**

LET ME TELL YOU a little bit about the Village and who hung out there. In the late fifties and early sixties, Greenwich Village was like no other place in the world. It was a magnet for artists, actors, singers, poets, writers, and musicians, along with a handful of uncommonly dedicated and ethical managers who believed in the power of the artists they represented. In other words, they were not interested in being stars themselves. There was also a clutch of the usual kind of cutthroat agents, but even these snakes had a certain amount of native charm. There was also a peripheral population of lunatics that, all combined, would go on to define a generation.

The swanky, uptown clubs were dissolving like the final

traces of an ice age. Upstairs at the Downstairs, Downstairs at the Upstairs, the Blue Angel, all those great clubs that featured cool pop, a tinkling piano, and highbrow sophistication by the early sixties had pretty much become pasteurized and homogenized like white milk. The reliance on overwitty, naughty, urbane lyrics gave these clubs a self-elected preeminence in New York's cultural refrigerator, where you could always open the door, no matter what the hour, and find something to ingest. The trouble was that no one was going out to these clubs anymore. What had changed?

People will give you many reasons. The old clientele was getting older, and club hopping is a young man's sport. Television began to take its toll. People were married with children now and couldn't afford the luxury. That is all true, but there was something odder. For some reason people just get bored with perfection. The fact that the most exquisite orchestral music was available before the turn of the twentieth century did not stop a new generation from preferring light opera and senti-mental concert pieces. When that kind of stuff became longhair and highbrow, Tin Pan Alley blossomed, and so did the musical show tradition and big bands. Nurtured by the movies and the cohesiveness of World War II, this sound became the music of the young. After the war, rhythm and blues and rock and roll began to evolve. By the fifties, a rough-hewn edge to entertain-ment was beginning to take hold. When you consider that Frank Sinatra and Tony Bennett were performing the repertoire of Cole Porter, Gershwin, and Rodgers and Hart, with the finest musi-cians available, arranged by the finest musical minds of their day like Nelson Riddle and Gordon Jenkins, and yet the number-one song on the hit parade was "Who's Sorry Now" done in one octave by Connie Francis with an arrangement that could have been scored by a high school marching band, it was clear that the times were changing. Each generation needs its own voice, and more than any other, this new generation was suspicious of slick professionalism. Actually, they were suspicious of everything. Showmanship and craftsmanship did not necessarily equal passion. Passion and truth meant that you maybe had to sweat and howl and croon about something besides the moon in June while you spoon.

Not only the music but also the comedy was becoming stale in these uptown clubs. Most of the comedians were from the stale end of the fifties, and the jokes were about mothers-in-law, crabgrass, and the suburbs. Who cared? In 1963 when the Blue Angel was dying of anemia, the owner, and my friend, Max Gordon, redesigned the interior of the club, changed the menu, and hired Woody Allen for the reopening. The place was mobbed. Audiences loved Woody's iconoclastic routines. A few weeks later, the engagement ended. Woody moved back downtown to the place that gave him his start, and the crowds followed. The Blue Angel finally closed for good. The place Woody moved back to, by the way, was the Bitter End.

In the fifties, the original iconoclasts were the beat poets. In the beginning, it was very much a literary scene in the Village. What eventually happened was that music slowly began to replace literature. Most particularly, folk music replaced poetry, not only in the Village but all over America. All the things that were not being said in the newspapers, on television, or in the popular magazines were being discussed in folk music. The real news was coming from poets who were setting their words to music or singing classics that resonated with meaning.

Just after the war, there were a few places that would book a folksinging act but not many. The Blue Angel and the uptown café society would occasionally hire people like Burl Ives and Paul Villard. In an early example of radical chic, some of the uptown clubs like the Rainbow Room actually booked Woody Guthrie and Leadbelly. The only downtown place that got in on the act was Max Gordon's Village Vanguard, but only infrequently. Max's place was almost exclusively jazz. Folk musicians mainly played for "causes" and benefits of one kind or another, and they usually involved labor unions. The pay wasn't great, but you could usually count on a few bucks and a meal.

Richard Dyer-Bennett and John Jacob Niles were the two most successful folksingers of the early era. They traveled around the country with whatever private or government funding they could acquire along with Josef Marais, who was a concert violinist and sang songs about the African veldt. Josh White, Burl Ives, and some others occasionally got on radio and early TV and even made the hit parade once or twice. But there was no real place for their young devotees to perform.

Then bit by bit espresso stands and cafés started to emerge. To increase business they would add entertainment. Art D'Lugoff opened the Village Gate, while little bars like Mike Porco's Folk City began popping up, and small clubs seemed to sprout out of basements like weeds. When I say small, I mean big enough to hold twenty or thirty people. It was like a big H, with Bleecker Street on the south and West Third Street on the north and MacDougal Street as the bar. By 1962, there must have been about fifty of these small places. Original music was somewhat rare, although there were many topical songs that lasted as long as yesterday's newspapers. Folk musicians mainly drew from the classic repertoire. Most of the singers were still doing the songs they sang for the unions and the strike lines.

Folk music existed happily in a kind of underground community. News and information traveled by word of mouth or small, rough-and-ready publications like *Sing Out!* and *Broadside* and through specialty shops like Izzy Young's Folklore Center.

When word got out about the great opportunities in Greenwich Village, coffeehouses started to open up all over the country. College campuses opened their stages for folksingers. Suddenly folk music was becoming vital.

During the fifties, there was a tremendous left-wing influence in the folk music world. I mean the Communist Party practically swallowed it up whole. Every event that was held, every fund-raiser, every strike, every picket line, every Communist Party meeting, every American Labor Party meeting, every lawyers' meeting, there had to be folksingers. It made the Communist Party sound like a New Year's Eve party. Come on, join the party. There will be music, wine, and free love. That kind of thing.

There was a little hall off Union Square where the first hootenannies were held. Oscar Brand was the first host. They would do programs with little tin-can microphones. Jean Ritchie appeared, the New Lost City Ramblers, Pete Seeger, of course, and Josh White, and they would do benefits for miners or to raise money for People's Songs, which was an organization started by Pete Seeger to promote folk music. There was always a cause to raise money for, there was always an audience, and the places would be packed. I don't know where the hell those people came from.

Then the little basement clubs took off, and those venues and club owners were capable of raising money and doing fund-raisers. A lot of these places didn't really put themselves out for the performers. You usually went in knowing you would be in a bad situation, with the roaches crawling around. There were always a lot of old refrigeration units in the basements of these places, and they were always dank and wet. Most of them had no place to just sit and be alone with your thoughts. One of the worst was one of the best clubs, the Village Vanguard, which catered mostly to jazz musicians, who were used to it. The only spots for performers were either at the tables drinking and smoking or being bought drinks or buying drinks. At the back entrance, the Vanguard had a little town house attached to it. There was a narrow stairway, and at the foot of the stairs was a little table about two feet wide. You sat on uncomfortable chairs, and there was no place to go.

Canada Lee, a black former boxer, used to recite Shakespeare there. He had been hit so many times he was almost blind, but he was a good actor. He played Caliban in a Broadway production of *The Tempest*. Burl Ives was a regular, and so was Richard Dyer-Bennett, until Burl ratted him out in the early days of the House Un-American Activities Committee hearings. John Carradine was also a regular; he recited Shakespeare and the most frightening horror poems. Albert Decker recited stories and poems by Edgar Allan Poe. Everybody called him PoeBoy. Paul Villard sat in the spotlight wearing a woolen sea cap and playing a concertina as he sang chanteys. But the Vanguard was a very important venue. Max Gordon was a pleasure, an honest, straightforward man who always paid the musicians. Sometimes in the jazz dives, that wasn't always the case. Most of the places, though, were just awful. If you were a performer, it wasn't the set itself that got you, it was the sitting around. This was the way it was when Fred Weintraub walked onto the scene.

Fred was born in the late twenties and was groomed from the beginning to take over the family baby-carriage business. He prepared for college at the Fieldstone School and later earned a degree in finance at the University of Pennsylvania's Wharton School of Business. Fred got married at age nineteen to a girl whose name he always claimed to have trouble remembering. It was Eleanor. They moved from the Bronx to Scarsdale, set up house, and had two children, both girls. Fred commuted to work every day. In the midst of all this seeming regularity, however, Weintraub was getting spiritually constipated. "You know why I married at nineteen?" Fred once asked. "I didn't know you could have an apartment of your own unless you got married. I thought you either got married or you lived with your mother. I was a real innocent. I was the kind of guy who fell in love with the local call girl."

The house in Scarsdale became a symbol for everything penitentiary, and the crabgrass on the lawn was a metaphor for the choke hold that life seemed to have on him. Finally, at the age of twenty-six, he woke up one morning, surveyed his kingdom, wife, kids, and crabgrass, and determined, like a male version of Nora in Ibsen's *Doll's House,* that the whole thing was crazy and left. "I was a typical middle-class boy who just got sick and tired of it all. I told myself, 'If this is my life then the hell with it.'"

Weintraub decided to wander. He headed for Europe and wandered around the Continent. He went to Israel and wandered some more. He finally wound up in Cuba. Rumor has it he bought into a kind of floating nightclub/whorehouse while playing piano on the side, inventing a whole crabgrass medley including variations on standards like "I Wonder Who's Picking It Now." It was in Cuba that the Weintraub "legend" was born. Bill Deseta, a former manager who ran the club in the early sixties, remembers many of the details.

Deseta says, "Fred's father owned a company that made baby furniture called the Darling Stores that started in the Bronx and eventually became a chain. And Fred, from when he was very young, worked at the store. He got married and had two daughters, one of whom, Sandy, went on to work in television production. One day he decided it was all too boring and left, walked out on the family, and went to Cuba. He got into business with some Cuban guy who owned a fishing boat. It turned out that the Cuban guy was running guns for Castro at night while Fred was running the fishing tours during the day. One night, Batista's troops came on the boat, took the guy out, and killed him. Since Fred was an American citizen and Batista was very friendly with the U.S., they decided not to shoot Fred and just sent him home."

Fred came back to New York around 1960 and started to hang out around the Village because it was fun and easy. Later he would claim not to know why he picked the Village as a hangout. "It's all very clear when you're young," he once said vaguely. He got a kick out of telling people he made his living as a chess shark at the Café Figaro espresso house and glommed his meals hunting up hotels where conventions were being held and then sitting himself down as a pretended delegate. He may well have won the chess matches and scammed the meals, but he didn't need the money.

Fred got a job with a small advertising agency, and he invented a way to sell television time that made the agency a ton of money. In those days, there was a kind of swindle that the manufacturers ran on the customers. Companies who sold goods to a retailer would give them, as part of a come-on, a television advertising credit. They told the retailers, "For every hundred thousand diapers you buy, we'll give you a credit worth twelve hundred dollars against the cost of a television commercial." The stores were never able to accumulate enough credits to actually take a commercial. Fred realized that all these credits were rolling around out there in never-never land, and he went out and put together twenty or so stores that sold the same product, got them to chip in their credits, and went out and bought a commercial with it. The commercial said, "In Newark you can get it at Blah Blah Blah! In Jersey City, you can get it at Blah Blah Blah!" He invented that style of advertising. Fred made a buck.

During his free time Fred would often hang out at a club on Bleecker Street called the Cock and Bull, which was run by Manny Roth. Manny was a writer and wanted to perform and produce his own shows. The Cock and Bull was originally used as a theater space. A young Dustin Hoffman played there when the little production he was in needed a restaurant setting. Occasionally guitar players could find work, and Fred used to hang out and play piano. Manny also owned the Café Wha? His nephew, David Lee Roth, did all right for himself too. Anyway, Fred wanted to break into the entertainment business and thought running a coffeehouse would be a good way to capitalize on the folk music boom that seemed to be infecting the country. It also seemed like an interesting thing to do at the time. He loved hanging out in Greenwich Village. "I get nervous," he once said, "anytime I'm above Fourteenth Street."

Like the new decade itself, everything seemed to be brand-new. With the world spinning faster and faster, it was easier to keep your balance at the center of things, and the bull's eye was Bleecker Street. The *Village Voice* was only five years old. If you were up at five in the morning, you could sometimes see novelist Norman Mailer driving around with copies of the *Voice*, which he helped found, in the backseat of his car, dropping them off at newsstands all over Lower Manhattan. Occasionally Mailer would write original pieces for the paper as well as producing advertisements for himself in the hopes of convincing people to buy his latest book.

Fred enjoyed hanging out and picking up girls. Making money was a sideline that he was awfully good at. Fred worked for the advertising company until he got bored with that game. He got bored because Fred got bored easily, and one day he simply walked out. He just walked away from the business. On June 6, 1961, Fred Weintraub went downtown, took the money he'd earned, and bought Manny's club. And that's how Fred joined the neighborhood and ended up with the Bitter End. But Fred was only one of many. Let me tell you a little about the other club owners and the men behind the artists. The Village was where the talent was, so it was only natural that the most brilliant and aggressive agents and managers would be downtown as well.

Art D'Lugoff started the Village Gate around 1955. He played folksingers and comedians, although the Gate was also very well known for its jazz acts. Art was also interested in avant-garde theater and produced a number of plays like *MacBird!* and *Jacques Brel Is Alive and Well.*

My good friend Harold Leventhal, who got me into this crazy business in the first place, practically set up camp. Harold's family was in ladies' garments and expected their son to follow in the business. Harold had other ideas. He loved the music of Woody Guthrie, the Almanac Singers, the Weavers, and Pete Seeger. Harold went on to manage all of them and then some. He loved the message that permeated their music: fairness, honesty, racial justice, and peace. In the beginning, his family was so adamant about him not entering show business that, for a while, Harold had to handle all the arrangements from behind the scenes while people like Pete Kameron actually acted the part whenever the spotlight was on or when there might be publicity, so Harold's family would be left in the dark. With the clientele that Harold represented, it didn't take long for his folks to acquiesce.

Harold told me that he would never audition people who came up to his business office. "I wanted to know, if I'm auditioning somebody, how do they work in front of an audience? How do they communicate in front of an audience? You can only do that with an audience. The Bitter End was the best place to find that out."

The Village was not only a good place to discover new talent but also a place where it was very easy to talk shop with other managers or to simply enjoy a show. Harold would go down to see Woody Allen. When Harold started out as a manager, he shared an office with Jack Rollins. Jack managed Woody, and Woody would come up to hang out or talk business. Jack Rollins and Charlie Joffe were downtown practically every night in the early sixties. They were marvelous agents who specialized in comedy. In the fifties Charlie and especially Jack were responsible for the success of Harry Belafonte as well as Mike Nichols and Elaine May. When Woody first approached Jack and Charlie, it was not about getting them to represent him as a stand-up comic. Woody wanted to write for Nichols and May. Mike and Elaine, however, wrote their own material. Harry Belafonte used to play the little jazz clubs until he got frustrated and quit. He tried running a hamburger joint until the place went bust and Harry was nearly broke. Jack found him and suggested he stop singing pop songs and do what Harry loved best, calypso. By the mid-fifties Harry Belafonte was making half a million bucks. Jack was also the first person to bring Lenny Bruce to New York City.

Throughout their careers Rollins and Joffe managed Woody Allen, Dick Cavett, Len Maxwell, Billy Crystal, and a singer named Danny Meehan, who may have been Jack and Charlie's only failure. Danny was a typical song-and-dance man. He wasn't really a Village-style act. In the early sixties, he was appearing on Broadway in *Funny Girl*. Since Fred was so close with Charlie and Jack, he wound up booking Danny at the Bitter End. Danny wore a straw hat and smoked cigarettes from a holder. Once when he was on the bill with Len Maxwell, he came into the dressing room after his set, flung his hat across the room, sat down, and said, "Len, I went out and gave them everything I had and they bought it." Len said, "Danny, if you ever get a TV show, your only sponsor should be Humble Oil."

Another manager-agent who set up shop in the Village was Albert Grossman. Albert was working for the Chicago Housing Authority when, in the late fifties, he caught the folk music bug. He became part owner, with Alan Rebeck, in a Chicago folksinging club called the Gate of Horn, where the two would sit around for hours drinking and singing sea chanteys. In the early sixties Albert moved his base of operations to the Village.

Albert created Peter, Paul and Mary, and at one time or another he managed Dylan, Odetta, the Band, Paul Butterfield, Richie Havens, Ian and Sylvia, Gordon Lightfoot, Janis Joplin, and Dr. John. He was one of the creators of the Newport Folk Festival and was a guiding force in insinuating electric music into the world of acoustic folk. It was a bitter pill for many to swallow. In 1965, folklorist Alan Lomax almost gagged when he had to introduce Paul Butterfield and his very electric Blues Band to the crowd at Newport. Lomax said, "Here's a band that's not very original, purely derivative. . . . I guess we'll just have to put up with them." It was such a snotty introduction that Albert Grossman went backstage, called Lomax a fucking idiot, and punched him in the nose. That was the year Dylan went electric and was almost booed off the stage. Pete Seeger tried to cut the electric cables with an ax. Everybody was a little uptight.

Albert hung out at the Bitter End all the time, especially when Peter, Paul and Mary were starting out. He also had a thing for one of the waitresses, Sally, whom he would later marry. Sally Grossman has the distinction of being one of two women who ever appeared on a Bob Dylan album cover. She is the severe-looking brunette on the cover of *Bringing It All Back Home*. Albert produced the classic *Don't Look Back*, a movie documentary of Dylan's England tour.

Roy Silver was also a presence, although not a happy one. When he wasn't stealing other men's wives, he was busy promoting himself as well as his acts, which he eventually would lose. He managed Bill Cosby until Bill discovered Roy was making things successful for Roy with Bill's money. He managed Joan Rivers until Joan discovered that Roy also wanted to be a star. Roy had a kind of moxie that was initially successful, but he would always blow it. Once when their respective acts were performing at the White House, Roy and Jack and Jane Rollins went to a presidential reception after the show. In the middle of the party, Roy grabbed Lyndon Johnson's arm, pushed him over toward Jack and Jane, and introduced him as if he were an old friend. After everybody shook hands and separated, Jane asked Roy if he knew the president. Roy said no, but he had a theory that presidents never carry any money and never know where they're going. Everything is done for them. So if you just walk over to them, grab their arm, and pull, they will likely follow because they'll assume you know what you're doing. Anyway, that was Roy.

When Sid Bernstein moved to the Village in 1963, he immediately got friendly with Fred Weintraub, and they hung out a lot together. One of Sid's best friends was my friend Billy Fields. When Billy finally threw his gloves in and gave up singing, it was Sid who got him a job managing the club and, a little later, helping with Fred's management company, Fredanna. Billy didn't like managing the Bitter End, so he wound up calling me. Whenever Sid heard a good act, he would let us know. Of course, about a year after he hit the area, February 12, 1964, he brought the Beatles to Carnegie Hall. They were a little too big for the Bitter End. But Paul McCartney's brother, Michael, played the club with his comedy troupe called the Scaffold, and we got to be good friends.

I know Sid eventually arranged Woody Allen's first Carnegie Hall date. Mel Tormé and Count Basie were the headliners. Inexplicably the show lost money. Woody got paid about seventy-five bucks. I think Sid lost more money than he made. Everybody grants him the Beatles, but few people realize that Sid brought not only the Beatles to America but also practically every other band that was part of the British Invasion.

Sid was another guy who cared intently about the music. For people like Sid, Art D'Lugoff, Albert Grossman, Harold Leventhal, Fred, and me, the music was the primary point; otherwise, we all would have sold shirts. It's just that along with this great love of the music, most of the other guys had a knack for making money. With Sid it was like alchemy in reverse. I know he was the first person to convince the old Madison Square Garden to produce rock and folk shows, and he began by booking Joan Baez. Sid wanted to charge twenty bucks a head and Joan said it was too much. She only wanted to charge five dollars or less. Without even doing the arithmetic, Sid said sure. He lost money. It was a great show, Joan was happy, the fans were happy, even Sid was happy, it's just that he lost money on the deal.

Sid remembers spending so much time at the Bitter End, hanging out and listening to the shows, that he often brought his young kids down to listen. "The feel of the place was actually very wholesome," he told me. "Kids from all over the United States used to come here. They would go back to their schools and talk about what they had seen. It helped a lot of acts find work. It was a great showcase."

Heavy-duty managers and promoters used to gather in a coffee klatch outside on the curb, talking business, leaning on the parked cars of the artists so they wouldn't get tickets. Club owners would be constantly checking out the competition. Art

D'Lugoff from the Village Gate; Howie Solomon from the Café Au Go Go; Manny Roth, who was concentrating on his other club, The Café Wha?; Sam Hood, who bought the Gaslight from John Mitchell. Any time of the evening you might see Woody Allen and Bill Cosby running into each other on their way to or from a set; Phil Ochs carrying his guitar and sheets and sheets of new songs stuffed into a brown grocery bag; Richie Havens and John Sebastian emerging from a tiny basket house with the five or ten dollars they had made. Jimi Hendrix had just come up from the south and was playing at the Café Au Go Go. He went under the name Jimmy James and the Blue Flames. Everybody wanted to see him. The streets were always flooded with people. Celebrities came down all the time, like Glynis Johns and Albert Finney, just to hang out and listen to the music. Singer-songwriter Jake Holmes told me that one night he came in late to see the show at the Au Go Go, which was right across the street from the Bitter End. When the show was over, he pushed the side doors open and walked out onto Bleecker Street. There were thousands of people clogging the street. When they saw the door open, they all sighed in expectation and then groaned when they saw Jake. Jake turned around and looked at the doors. Again they opened. Again the sigh and the groan, but this time Paul Newman and Joanne Woodward walked out. Now Jake was really interested. The doors finally opened again, and out walked Richard Burton and Elizabeth Taylor, and the crowd went crazy.

Anyway, that was the Village back then, and those were some of the players. It didn't take long before the whole world caught on to what was happening.

3

THE GREAT FOLK MUSIC SCARE OF THE SIXTIES

Folk music goes in and out of fashion. When folk music is not in fashion, it is always there on obscure labels in specialist shops for those who want it, and those who do not want it are people who have no souls.

—**Donald Clarke,** *The Rise and Fall of Popular Music*

BY 1961, IN THE VILLAGE the literary scene was waning. There was still a bunch of magazine writers hanging out in the bars, but the novelists were gone. They had gotten old or were doing other things, or else they were slumming on television. Most of the beats either were dead or had moved to the West Coast. A lot of the hangers-on were still hanging around, but they weren't talented, they just looked the part. They were becoming caricatures of the original beats. In fact, by the late fifties, they were being called beatniks. After the Russians launched the Sputnik satellite, everybody started pinning the suffix "nik" onto the end of words like the tail on a donkey. It became a national joke, like Tom Swifties. So if you were in favor of nuclear disarmament, you became a "peacenik"; if you were a crummy person, you became a "no-goodnik." That's how the beats became beatniks.

There was one thing that was hot, however, and getting hotter: folk music. Every Sunday, Washington Square Park would be filled with young street musicians who would practice all week and then come to the park to see if they could sing and play in front of people. The Village locals hated it and sent the cops to arrest the singers. It became a volatile political issue. I remember when Ed Koch, who was just getting into politics at the time and was running for Congress in the Village district, tried to get the singers out of the park. There were even a couple of miniriots. The *Village Voice*, which was about twenty pages long, took the side of the musicians. Eventually the singers won out. Folk music organizations began springing up. The most famous was Israel Young's Folklore Center on Mac-Dougal Street.

What eventually happened was that all these little poetry clubs in the neighborhood ran out of poets. So they started hiring folksingers. The funny thing was that the beats never really liked folk music very much. Most of them liked cool jazz, hard drugs, and existentialism. The folkies were very optimistic. They thought they could change the world with a song. The beats' message was "Shoot up, stay stoned, and wait for Armageddon." Before folk music became dominant and there was still an audience for poetry, it was funny to watch the reaction. If a folkie came up between two beat poets, the audience would usually hold their collective nose or stick napkins in their ears.

Summer nights in the Village back then were just incredible. Bleecker Street was packed with people. There were the locals, and a lot of them were in gangs, and they hated all the straggly artist types. There were the straggly artists who were pouring in from all over the country, and there were throngs of tourists. Crowds overflowed from the shops and the cafés onto the streets because the pavements couldn't accommodate them. They all wanted to come to the Village and see the beatniks and hear their dirty poems. What they got instead was folk music.

This only increased the tension between the coffeehouse owners and the locals. This led to some funny accommodations. In some of the clubs, like the Gaslight, the heating system was so antiquated that all the open ducts ran from the cellar, where the club was, up the building and into the apartments above. And music just tended to be louder than a lone poet reciting his angst. The sound of applause was louder still. It traveled right up into the apartments and drove the tenants crazy. It got so bad that after a certain hour the audience wasn't allowed to clap. They had to snap their fingers to show approval. The whole idea of finger-snapping beatniks became a joke and wound up in TV shows and movies. It was supposed to be the ultimate in laid-back, hip response. It was really because John Mitchell, who owned the Gaslight, was too lazy to plug up the holes in the basement.

When Manny Roth still owned 147 Bleecker Street, it was known as a base of operations for Mark Spoelstra, a popular twelve-string guitarist who played and sang the blues à la Leadbelly. It was really nothing more than a hole in the wall. When Fred walked in and told Manny he wanted to buy the place, Manny actually thought he had found a sucker.

Fred decided to rename the club the Bitter End. In the summer of 1961, that entire area of Bleecker Street was pretty close to a slum. The Bitter End was the last club on Bleecker Street.

There was a bar right next door called the Dugout. It was a beer-and-ball dive. If you pass 147 Bleecker Street now, you run into the campus of NYU, but back then there was nothing. All the winos would spend their day begging in the Village and then take whatever money they made and hang out at the Dugout. So it was their last stop too. Then they would walk across the street to the Bowery and flop. The Bitter End was the perfect name because it was the last "normal" place on Bleecker Street. It was the last stop before you got to desolation.

Fred spent a lot of money fixing the place up. The first thing he did was strip off all the plaster, leaving the bare red brick walls. It was a stroke of genius. That red brick wall motif became the backdrop for musical and comedy clubs for the next thirty-five years. Everybody has used the milieu at one time or another. The nation got a chance to see it when the first Peter, Paul and Mary album came out. The cover was shot on stage at the Bitter End, and since the album has never gone out of print, you can still see it today. The Bitter End started getting featured in national magazines and always with the red brick wall in the background. People in Idaho started peeling the plaster off their walls.

The red brick wall for some reason just gave the place a hip feel. The rest of the walls were lined with copies of lithographs by Max Ernst. There was a smashed-up piano clinging to a piece of wall that was part of the work of an artist who did what he called destruction art. This guy would destroy somebody else's work of art, and that became his art. Fred put little signs all over the place with proverbs from the Weintraub School of Philosophy: "One good mistress deserves another." "Beat your mother while she's young." "He who bestirs himself is lost." "Cold meat lights no fire."

As you walked into the club, the stage was on the right-hand side, about ten inches off the ground. It is still like that today. There were church pews to the left where the audience sat. The pews were the kind with wooden backs, and the backs had ledges on them where you could rest your hymnbooks. The ledges became the tables for the sodas and ice-cream drinks that were all that could be served since there was no liquor license. It would also hold the ashtrays and the clay flowerpots that were used as ice buckets. It all had a beat-generation feel to it, and the people loved it.

Fred started to build his staff. He hired a comedian named Murray Roman to act as emcee. Murray was a hipster who tried very hard to carry the Lenny Bruce torch into the seventies. He always made the delivery jive and could be counted on to squeeze the word "groovy" into every sentence four or five times. He got on TV every once in a while and had a pretty successful tour with the Baja Marimba Band in the mid-sixties. He even made a couple albums. The English rockers called him the "inappropriate comic." Murray, offstage, at a table, was one of the funniest guys in the world. You could fall on the floor. But if you put him onstage, he iced an audience. He froze. He got classic flop sweat. He had one routine where he compared the three kinds of highs that guys get when they try to pick up girls. The booze high was, "Hey, baby, you got a nice ass." The pot high was, "Oh, baby, you are so groovy I want to get inside your spirit." And the acid high was, "Excuse me, are you a guy or a chick?"

Fred hired a couple of young guys to run the lights and manage the kitchen, usually simultaneously. Jon Gibbs was the sound and lighting man. Jon lived on Thompson Street around the corner from the club. At one point Jon had actually run an electrical line from the back door of the Bitter End across the yards, up to his apartment. The idea was that artists, in between sets, could hang out at Jon's apartment because the dressing room was very small. With the line activated, you could always know what was going on onstage.

Adam Perelman, the son of writer S. J. Perelman, was hired as a sort of house manager. But there was no real hierarchy. Fred was the owner, but he was really the dictator, and the help did what he said. If there was a problem anywhere, he would point and say, "Adam, we need toilet paper in the ladies' room." Or, "Jon, go and borrow ten pounds of coffee from Manny at the Cafe Wha?"

The very first acts to play the Bitter End included an area duo that called themselves the Trav-Lers; a beat poet named Hugh Romney, who later changed his name to Wavy Gravy; and a black folksinger named Len Chandler. The Trav-Lers were the opening act, Hugh Romney was the "comic," and Len Chandler was the headliner.

Dick Reicheg of the Trav-Lers remembers the pre–Wavy Gravy well. "I ran into Hugh on the street one day, and he had just gotten a job doing a concert somewhere uptown. Something fancy. He told me he was going to wear his 'meat jacket.' I said, 'What's a meat jacket?' Hugh said, 'I took a sports coat and sewed cold cuts into it—pastrami, salami, corned beef, some cheese.' I said, 'Wow, I never heard of that before.' He said, 'I know it's going to be great.' I ran into him a couple of days later and I asked him how the show went. He said, 'Great, except the salami curled under the lights.'"

Once, a guy walked up to Hugh on the street with a bunch of pills. The guy said, "Hugh, you know about this shit. What kind of pills are these and what will they do?" Hugh took them in his hand, studied them for a second, and swallowed the whole bunch. "I'll let you know in an hour," he said.

As a beat, Hugh published some remarkable and beautiful

poems, but eventually he transformed himself into a kind of clown prince. It was actually B. B. King who rechristened Hugh Wavy Gravy, a baptism many people feel was B. B.'s revenge on the white man.

One night, after the premiere show, Len Chandler saw a bunch of street kids beating up a black guy with bats. He yelled at them to stop, but instead of stopping, they ran after Len with the bats. Len hightailed it back to the Bitter End and ran inside just as Fred was getting ready to close. Fred walked out and tried to reason with the kids until one of them hit Fred over the head with the bat and smashed the windows of the club. Len got away, but they had to take Fred to the hospital for stitches. The early sixties in the Village were not all about peace and love.

By Labor Day Fred had worked out a deal with Albert Grossman to have Grossman's new act, Peter, Paul and Mary, take over the club. Grossman had been trying to put together a folk group act for a while. He initially wanted to build it around Bob Gibson. He had already paired Bob Gibson with Hamilton "Bob" Camp, and the two of them recorded a very successful live album from the Gate of Horn in Chicago. But Gibson and Camp were erratic and hard to handle.

Grossman first heard of Peter Yarrow at the Cafe Wha? early in 1960 and decided to manage him. Noel "Paul" Stookey was a very usable emcee and comedian and worked all over the Village. But Noel wasn't Grossman's first choice. He approached Logan English, and Logan said no. He tried to recruit Dave Van Ronk, who also said no. Dave told me later that if he had ever gotten involved, he would have sunk the group like a millstone. They found Mary Travers at Izzy Young's Folklore Center.

Izzy wasn't much of a businessman, but his shop was the center of all the musical action in the Village. It was successful in spite of Izzy. He was eccentric but very passionate about the music. Occasionally, in moments of whimsy, he would put on lederhosen, grab some bells, and step dance down MacDougal Street, German style, in the middle of the afternoon. He wouldn't even bother to lock the store.

Peter Yarrow went in to buy guitar strings one day and saw a picture on the wall. Peter said, "Oh my God, who's that?" Izzy said, "That's Mary Travers. She'd be great if you could get her to work."

Peter was never sure what Izzy meant by that, but they all finally got together at Mary's apartment and harmonized on "Mary Had a Little Lamb." Magic was in the air. Peter told me later it was unmistakable. "It was the same kind of extraordinary bolt of lightning that you have when you fall in love with somebody and you say, 'That's my person!' and indeed it turns out to be. That's how much I knew that this was it."

They rehearsed for about seven months at Mary's apartment. The owner of the Fat Black Pussycat let Peter and Noel eat there every night, since they hadn't a penny to their name. Peter only owned a single pair of green corduroy pants. Finally, Grossman tried them out at Gerde's Folk City, but the response was not warm. They were taking their baby steps. Then they came to the Bitter End.

One of their problems was that they didn't have a lot of material. That should have been a hindrance, but it wasn't. Each was an artist in his own right. Peter had played at Newport the year before. He had charisma. There was something about him that just riveted your attention to him. And Noel was just the sweetest guy in the world and very, very funny. Mary could sing like a bird, and she had the most fantastic look. It defined the sixties.

They decided to open their show with Peter doing a solo act for about fifteen minutes. One of his opening songs was "Buddy

Can You Spare a Dime?" To this day, Peter does one of the most impassioned versions of that song you'll ever hear. Then Noel, who was now called Paul, which was his middle name anyway, did his stand-up routine. Noel was so funny it hurt. He could do imitations like the old flush toilet at Carnegie Hall. We did a benefit years later at the Bitter End, and Noel got up and did the toilet routine. Nobody in the audience ever heard it before except Peter, Mary, and me. Noel had them rolling in the aisles.

His coup de grace was a routine about his college days in Michigan. There was a football player named Bruno who lived in one of the dorms. Bruno made long-distance phone calls every weekend, and it never cost him a dime. Noel suspected that the swindle was part of the guy's athletic scholarship because Noel believed old Bruno could never have figured out how to do it himself. It revolved around a hanger that was bent in a crazy way, and Bruno carried it in a violin case, like a tommy gun, with the hanger outline carved out of the velvet.

This guy would come out carrying this case, and the entire dorm would be galvanized, and the whisper would be, "Hey, Bruno's gonna make a phone call." Bruno would ceremoniously take this hanger device out of the case and stick it into the coin-return slot. Then he would turn and twist it into the interior of the phone until there was nothing left but a small piece of wire about the size of a cigarette butt. Then he would dial the number of his girlfriend, and the operator would say, "That will be your entire life savings, pleeyays."

Noel continued with the bit describing how Bruno would take this immense bag of quarters and drop the coins in, one by one, all the while imitating the sound of the coins falling into the maw of the telephone. Cluschedingk! Cluschedingk! Then he would talk to his girlfriend for an hour and finally hang up the phone. Well, in those days, when you hung up the phone, after putting in a lot of change, it would go "ca-ching" and the money would settle into the box. But instead of "ca-ching," you would just hear the "ca"—the "ching" wouldn't happen.

Then Bruno would turn the hanger in the opposite direction, and bit by bit it would emerge from the coin-return slot. Finally, with a flourish, Bruno would pull it completely out, and it would be like jackpot time in Vegas. All the quarters would gush out, and the entire dorm burst into cheers as if Bruno had just made an end run for a touchdown. It was one of the highlights of his college education.

Then the three of them, Peter, Paul, and Mary, would close the show, and the magic was so palpable you could see it through the cigarette smoke. But the response wasn't instantaneous. Through the first week the response was not good. So the Bitter End took out an ad in the *New York Times:* "If you are a collector of rare type ads then go and cut this one out. I am in no way connected with a club operating under the name of the Bitter End. But last weekend I saw an act there that I'd just like to tell you about." The ad went on to talk about Peter, Paul and Mary and the club. "You better see this trio before you have to pay fancy uptown prices at the Blue Angel," it continued. "You better see them fast."

The following weekend the crowds picked up some, but it wasn't exactly devastating. It wasn't huge. The next weekend the club took out another ad: "For all you people who responded to the idiot who wrote this bizarre ad last week, I'd like to apologize. And I'd like to apologize to all the people who came down to the Bitter End and were not able to get in. Too many tourists. If you really want to see this incredible new act, I recommend you make reservations during the week. We are going to expand the premises to accommodate more of you."

That was the second ad. The following weekend it rained,

and Fred had to hire people to go out in the street and hold umbrellas over the heads of customers who were standing in line. After that there was no looking back. Peter, Paul and Mary became one of the most emblematic singing groups of the sixties. They have been unbelievably successful. They have played for free and for benefits probably as many times as they have played for money. They have made over fifty albums among them, but their first one will always by my favorite. It's a gem, and so are they. Peter told me many times that it was the Bitter End that made their career. "Playing the Bitter End was like playing the Palace."

Toward the end of 1961, more young singers, such as Tom Paxton, came looking for work. Tom played the club with a popular guitarron player named Gil Robbins. A guitarron is a big-body guitar that acts like a stand-up bass. Gil Robbins is the father of the actor Tim Robbins. Another big Village guitarron player who was always around was Felix Pappalardi. At the Bitter End, Felix often backed up Fred Neil, but his main partner was Lou Gossett Jr. Lou was doing a play at the time called *The Blacks* by Jean Genet, in which he also played and sang. Many actors took advantage of the folk music boom to supplement their income, like Alan Arkin, Leon Bibb, and Theo Bikel. Folk songs generally told a story, and what better interpreter of a story could you have than a trained actor?

By 1962, thanks to the national success of Peter, Paul and Mary and the fact that their album was number one on the charts, the Bitter End was established as the country's premier coffeehouse. One of the natural offshoots of that fact was that artists and agents and producers wanted to make live records from the club. This would be the beginning of a long series of hit albums recorded "live from the Bitter End." A short list of artists who made records here includes Fred Neil, the Chad

Mitchell Trio, Pete Seeger, the Tarriers, Bill Cosby, Donny Hath-away, Ellen McIlwaine, Curtis Mayfield, David Steinberg, Eric Andersen, Arlo Guthrie, Biff Rose, Randy Newman, Len Chandler, Jo Mapes, Mike Settle, Art and Happy Traum, Tom Paxton, Bill Haley and the Comets, Tommy James and the Shondells, and the Isley Brothers. The only other places that have more recording credits are the Village Gate and Carnegie Hall.

In the fifties and early sixties, the most influential folksinger, outside of Pete Seeger, was Bob Gibson. Many people may have forgotten Bob, but it is impossible to overestimate his influence. His CDs are available, and he made a few live recordings from the Bitter End on compilation albums, so his work is out there if anyone wants to listen. Gibson had some of the greatest pop music sensibilities of anybody.

Bobby Gibson was the Frank Sinatra of folk music. He was the guy who brought it uptown. The original folkies were one guitar and three chords. Gibson changed all that. He could take the traditional words of a folk song and add harmonies and chord progressions that could stun an audience into amazement. He had an enormous influence on Judy Collins, Joni Mitchell, and Phil Ochs especially. Phil and Bob wrote a lot of songs together; in fact, that's how Phil learned to write much of his best work. Gibson also worked closely with Shel Silverstein, and you have to have a great sense of humor to do that. Bob Gibson helped shape a lot of the popular music of the period.

Bob Gibson was also a heavy drug user, and it is amazing how he managed to keep his career going at all. He was his own worst enemy. Once he was doing a show at the club, and he was out of it. What killed Bob was that he was so damn good that it didn't matter. Even when he could barely sing three notes, he could still kill an audience. On this particular night he was going to do one of the traditional songs, "John Henry" or "My Dog

Blue," it doesn't matter which one, because the high point of the song was the introduction. He had a twenty-minute intro to the song, and it was very, very funny. It was all based on timing and on a bad opening line. Johnny Carson used to be famous for that technique. Carson would make a bad joke, wait until the audience groaned, and then come back with a string of funny, ad-lib follow-ups. The real jokes are the ad-libs, but the routine has to seem extemporaneous, otherwise it bombs.

So Bob does this routine. He makes a couple of blunders and the audience laughs, and then he goes off on this speculative monologue that is very funny. His timing is perfect. The room is packed, and they're falling out of the pews. It was very entertaining. And then he went into his version of "John Henry." He gets a great ovation. Now, he's standing on stage, tuning his guitar, and he sort of mumbles, "I wonder what I'm going to sing next?" Some joker in the audience yells out, "Do 'John Henry'!" which is the song he just finished. Bob was so fucked up, he just bounced right back into the beautifully timed introduction that was so funny because it seemed off the cuff. The audience was appalled. For another twenty minutes the people just sat there, stunned, as he went through all the cute remarks that they had just heard and had been entertained by, except now there is a deathly pall over the room. Nobody laughed. Bob was so out of it, he didn't care. When he got offstage, he told one of the waitresses that this audience wasn't as hip as the last one.

Of course all the best acts had little tricks. Josh White played the club, and sometimes when he thought he was losing the audience, he would break a string on his guitar. It looked accidental, but he actually pulled on it until it snapped. Then he'd apologize, take the string off, and put a new one on, but all the while, he would talk. He could tell any number of stories, but it would always end with a story about bringing the guitar into tune. Then he would complete the story exactly as he brought the guitar into perfect pitch and would go right into a song. Toward the end of his career, instead of yelling a request for a song, some of his devotees would yell, "Break a string!" It had become the best part of the act.

Sometimes we featured Bob Gibson, but we also used him a lot as an emcee. Emcees only had to sing a few songs or tell a few jokes and then introduce whoever was on the bill. Ed McCurdy was a big emcee for us when the club first opened. Ed was a straightforward baritone and a great interpreter of the old songs. "There once was a girl from so-and-so who did such-and-such with so-and-so." He sang a lot of "ribald" songs and "bawdy" songs, that kind of thing. He did have a pretty good sense of humor. Ed once met the brilliant pianist Glenn Gould. Gould was very strange. He never liked to shake hands with people. He met McCurdy, and Ed warmly stuck out his hand, and Gould said, "Oh, I'm so sorry, I hope you don't mind if we don't shake hands; you see I'm a pianist." So McCurdy mimicked him and said, "Oh, that's all right. I hope you don't mind if we don't kiss. I'm a singer." McCurdy was the author of "Last Night I Had the Strangest Dream," which was a great end-of-the-evening-round-the-campfire song. It was the original "Give Peace a Chance."

Oscar Brand played the club a lot back then. Oscar has done more work in more ways than anyone I know. He's a singer, musician, songwriter, artist, author, producer, actor, disc jockey, playwright, and psychiatrist. Ed McCurdy and Oscar were part of the Pete Seeger generation. They were a little solemn for the sixties and treated the music very reverently. Oscar told me he often saw Noel Stookey perform before he got with Peter, Paul and Mary and would get annoyed because Noel would say things about the songs that weren't true. Woody Guthrie was a particularly close friend, and Noel did a number of Woody's songs in a somewhat silly way, but he would never mention that the songs were written for children. "Well," Noel would say, "this song is distinguished as being one of the stupidest songs you ever heard." It was just a joke, but to Oscar it was like farting in church. There was a song about a disaster at sea, I forget what it was called, "The Wreck of the Good Ship Cockamamie," something like that. There were a million of those songs. But it was very tragic and solemn. Noel would sing it straight until he got to the chorus and then do a lot of glug-glug-glugs as the ship was sinking. It was a riot. A lot of the young acts would often make fun of the old songs and sing them as parodies.

I know Oscar would get revenge sometimes because he had his radio show, which is still on the air. Oscar won a Peabody Award recently for the longest-running folk music program in the history of the medium. He would invite some of the young acts on who did folk music comedy. They would sing a song and do a short interview, but Oscar wouldn't be there. The producer would ask the questions and explain that Oscar would come in later on and they would edit in the questions. But Oscar wouldn't ask the same questions. He would change them a little so the answers would sound stupid.

It was right around this time that a lot of little innovations were going on. They seem so obvious now, but back in 1962 the Bitter End and some of the other Village clubs were leading the way in sound and lighting. At the very beginning, when Peter, Paul and Mary first started, there was no lighting board or sound system. There was originally only one microphone, and Peter and Noel would sort of lean in and out as they sang. Because Peter was so much shorter than Noel, Noel always had to lean down, and the two of them did a balancing act. Tom Paxton recently recalled the day somebody in the club put up a guitar mike. No one had ever done that before. It was like the theatrical equivalent of quantum mechanics. Before that, the singer would sing then step back and kind of lift his guitar up to the microphone.

In the middle of Peter, Paul and Mary's engagement, Fred set up a series of lights that could be controlled by individual switches. I don't know if it was his idea or Albert Grossman's, but they wanted some sort of mood lighting. I think there was a blue light and a white one and a couple that were gelled to create different moods. You had to hit all three switches down at the same time to get a blackout. Chip Monck, who was the stage manager at the Village Gate, invented most of this. The Bitter End's lighting man, Jon Gibbs, was Chip's protégé. Edward Herbert Beresford "Chip" Monck. Nobody knows his first and middle names. If you ever heard the record of Woodstock, Chip is the emcee warning the people about the bad acid or dope that was going around. That was Chip.

There were very few acts back then that would qualify as virtuosos. This goes back to what I said earlier about rejecting professionalism. Uptown society, of course, was different, but this was downtown, and there wasn't a whole lot of show business savvy. I remember when Juan Serrano, the brilliant flamenco guitarist, played the club. Theo Bikel was wild about him and got Harold Leventhal to manage him. He played the Bitter End on numerous occasions. He was as good as Segovia. The young folkies would sing a song that might require three or four chords on the guitar. Juan Serrano would get up and play every conceivable note on the guitar in about forty seconds. After each set the folkies would go in the back room and put their guitars in the case or lean them up against a wall. Juan would get a little screwdriver and adjust the tuner. He would get a dust cloth and stroke the wood. He would dab the cloth in solution and rub the strings and the soundboard. The young guys would watch him in awe. They would look at each other and say, "Gee, maybe we should be doing this with our guitars." Everyone was learning everything all at once.

The politics of the day were crazy. The Bay of Pigs disaster had happened, and nuclear war was a real possibility. Nuclear radiation and fallout were hot-button issues. Mort Sahl used to do a routine about Japanese tourists visiting the West Coast and watching TV and seeing A-bomb tests being done in the Nevada desert. Then they would change channels and pick up Walt Disney's Mouseketeers show and freak out because all the kids were running around with rodent ears. It was scary, but it was great ammunition for guys like Pete Seeger and his protégés. In February 1962, I recall watching one of the first peace rallies in New York. About fifty people showed up, and there were even some arrests. Not a big turnout, but the movement would grow, thanks in part to people like Pete.

Pete Seeger had an apartment on MacDougal Street. As Woody Guthrie began to succumb to Huntington's disease, Pete was more or less enthroned as the titular head of the folk music community and the progressive way of life. Hating Pete Seeger was a cottage industry for certain people back in the fifties and early sixties. Because Pete refused to name names during the McCarthy hearings, he was convicted of contempt of Congress and sentenced to ten years in jail. A lot of people forget that. Pete's manager, Harold Leventhal, ran fund-raisers at the club for his legal bills. They were called "For Pete's Sake."

People hated Pete so much that they became stupid. The story was always the same. Pete and his songs and the message they portrayed were dangerous. The Establishment's energies were so concentrated on getting at Pete that they couldn't see what was happening right under their noses. Groups like the

Kingston Trio took Pete's songs and made them top-forty hits. These kids were so all-American looking with their crew cuts and fraternity sweaters that it was impossible to blacklist them. It was all a façade and highly hypocritical.

One of the first live recordings at the Bitter End was done by the Chad Mitchell Trio. They were led by Chadbourne Mitchell III and were encouraged into performing by one of the faculty clergy, a Father Beaver, from Gonzaga University, who not only ran the glee club but also doubled as an army chaplain. Gonzaga was Bing Crosby's alma mater, for God's sake. How American can you get? So while Pete was busy getting beat up by the Legion of Americanism, acts like the Chad Mitchell Trio were traveling all over the country singing Pete Seeger and Woody Guthrie songs, not to mention union protest songs and Russian love ballads, with impunity.

Chad Mitchell Trio: Live from the Bitter End was a great album. The boys didn't play any instruments themselves, so they hired backup musicians. Fred Hellerman of the Weavers was on guitar. Jim McGuinn, who would later change his name to Roger and become a founding member of the Byrds, played guitar and banjo. Roger and the Byrds would also have major hits written by Pete. Spike Lee's dad, Bill Lee, played bass. Bill Lee played at the club for years as backup for a lot of acts, including the Womenfolk and Ronnie Gilbert. Harry Belafonte's production company produced the whole show.

Chad Mitchell's opening number was "The John Birch Society," which was so topical that most people wouldn't get the jokes today, especially the references to Westbrook Pegler and Pinky Lee, but the hip, well-read audiences at the Bitter End loved it. When the record came out, the large radio stations in the country tried to ban that song. The advertisers were under the thumb of the Legion of Americanism, and they put the pressure on, but the small independent stations played it. There were so many infuriated calls in protest to the blackout that the most popular disc jockey in New York at the time, William B. Williams of WNEW, had to list the sponsors over the air so the protesters could blackball *them*!

Pete always performed at the larger-than-coffeehouse venues in and around New York. But in January 1962, there was a special performance at the Bitter End to record one of his best albums, *The Bitter and the Sweet*.

Overall, they were still innocent days. In the summer the Bitter End ran hootenannies on the Hudson River Dayliner, and there were plenty of parties. A lot of the other club owners like Art D'Lugoff and Manny Roth came along. Dave Van Ronk played, and so did Jo Mapes and Cynthia Gooding. We always had Oscar Brand on board because the amplification was in short supply and Oscar had the loudest voice. There was food and drink and sing-alongs on each deck, and the music carried sweetly across the Hudson River. Hootenannies were always great fun until Fred decided to get the club involved in a TV version. And, brother, was there hell to pay for that one.

4

WHAT'S A HOOTENANNY?

All music is folk music. I ain't never heard
no horse sing a song.

—Louis Armstrong

THERE ARE MANY STORIES about how the word "hootenanny" was born. The liner notes on old folk albums sometimes say it started as a joke: What happens when you cross an owl with a goat? But that makes it seem like nothing more than cacophony. It was more than that.

There was another story that said it went back to sing-alongs at Hoot Gibson's house. Hoot and his wife, Annie, would throw weekend parties, and if you wanted to hang out, you said you were going to Hoot and Annie's. That certainly was cute.

The truth is more prosaic. Pete Seeger brought the term back from the Northwest when he traveled there after World War II with Woody Guthrie and the remnants of the Almanac Singers. Hootenannies, wingdings, sing-alongs. They all meant the same thing. But it was Pete who brought the term back across America to the East Coast, and the name stuck. Of course

Pete would never formally take credit for it, but that was Pete. In the Greenwich Village coffeehouses the name was usually shortened to "hoots." At the Bitter End and the rest of the Village clubs, "hoot night" meant amateur night.

During the midweek and on weekends, if you had a decent lineup of talent, it wasn't hard to fill the house. But Mondays and Tuesdays were usually pretty slow nights. On Mondays some of the clubs were dark. And you had to give the headliners a night or two off. All through the sixties and seventies, when acts would play the Bitter End for a week's run, that usually meant a minimum of fourteen shows, at least two sets during midweek and three on the weekends—more if we could squeeze them in. The shows always had a real vaudeville feel to them. There was always an opening act, a comedian, and a headliner. Then, clear the house and start again. There was always a need for talent, especially for the warm-up spot. That's what the hoots were for.

The hoots were a way to keep the talent pool fresh and keep the clubs humming during the slow period. The uptown clubs held auditions during the day. The only audience was the owners or the music director. When we held auditions, we charged the public to come and listen too. Actually, there was nominally a quick look to make sure the amateurs weren't hideous. But if you had one or two good songs in you, there was a good chance you would get on. This was incredibly helpful for not only the clubs but also the agents and recording honchos, because the Village was brimming with talent. It was exciting because you never knew who the next star would be or when he or she would walk onstage.

A moderator always ran the hoots. At one time or another, comedian Murray Roman; folksingers Logan English, Ed McCurdy, Bob Gibson; George Terry, one of the founders of the Ace Trucking Company; and many more helped organize and run the hoots. We had a big handsome guy named Jack Knight who did it for a while. Jack was also the club bouncer and was more interested in sports than music or comedy. When he relocated to California, he was often found at the Improv and the Comedy Store acting like the house heckler. He later wound up on the TV hit *Cheers* as one of the regulars at the bar. After the softball pitching ace who traveled the country as the King and His Court retired, Jack took his place. He finally made it in sports.

There were always a lot of acts that wanted to be on for hoot night, and somebody had to show up and listen to them to see if they were stageworthy. It was a hard job. You had young people from all over the country traveling to be on the Bitter End hoot. The moderator had to play God, which was not a position anyone really enjoyed. There were comics who were not funny, singers who couldn't hold a note, and musicians who couldn't play their instruments. Often you would have to listen to a lot of what we called Joanie Phonies or Joanie Clonies, the girls with the nylon-string guitars and the long straight hair who knew the whole Joan Baez songbook in the key of C. If somebody was really bad, if their guitar was out of tune and they didn't know how to get it back in tune, if they were dreadful, well, you would have to weed them out. You would tell them they would have to work on their material and to come back in a couple of weeks. Every once in a while you had to pick the best of the worst because the pickings were slim. They were usually the acts that went on late.

Dick Reicheg was a Village regular and, as I mentioned, had the distinction of being one of the first performers who ever appeared at the Bitter End. He was in a folk act named the Trav-Lers and later played as a duo with comedy writer Lenny Levine as Lenny and Dick. When Dick went solo, he moderated the hoots for a year or so.

He recalled this story recently: "Once there was a young guy with a terrible haircut. The hair was important in those days. He came in with a guitar and he had glasses and he looked like a nerd. He took out the guitar, and my reaction, before he played, was 'This is not going to be so good.' He picked up the guitar in the dressing room and he started to play unbelievably great. He was astounding. Never seen him before. Never seen him around the Village. I said. 'You're on, man. I'm giving you the 9:30 slot,' which was prime time. 'What's your name?' 'David Bromberg. I'm in the army and I'm stationed on the East Coast. Close enough to take a bus in.' I'm sure that was David's first appearance in New York. He had it all together. He was just up and down the neck of the guitar."

Another guy who ran the hoots was Richmond Shepard. At the time he was Lionel Shepard. It seemed like everybody was changing his first name back then. Bobby Camp became Hamilton Camp. Jimmy Gavin became Weston Gavin. Jim McGuinn became Roger McGuinn. Go figure. Richmond ran a mime troupe, and he often did a show at the club called the Mime and Me. Mike Mislove was twelve years old when he started with Richmond. Mike was another founding member of the Ace Trucking Company. Lily Tomlin got her first Equity card with Richmond's troupe. One night a young woman comes in dragging a blind Puerto Rican kid by the hand. The kid had a guitar. The woman told Richmond, "Put him on the stage; he's really good." Richmond said, "Yeah, sure." I put him on at two o'clock in the morning after everyone else. It was José Feliciano. Soon as I heard him sing, I grabbed her and said, "Listen, you bring him in anytime you want. Give me three minutes notice, and he goes on next. Whatever you want, you got it."

José had a number he always did at the club called "The Flight of the Bumblebee." He played it so fast and so perfectly that the audience would just marvel, like they had seen something supernatural. We had to put him on at the end of every show because the other acts never wanted to follow him. Nobody in the record industry picked him up right away, which was crazy but good for us. Very often a performer would show up drunk or not show up at all, and we would need replacements fast. Once one of the house managers, David Wilkes, who is now an A&R, or artist and repertoire, man for Mercury Records, had to find somebody fast. Somebody billed to play had just called and said he fell asleep on the bus and just woke up. In Connecticut. So Dave went over to Gerde's Folk City and said, "Is anyone around?" Mike Porco said, "I think José is in the men's room." When Wilkes went in, José was at a urinal and his dog was with him. Big German shepherd. Dave stood next to José and said, "Hey man, you want to make a quick twenty-five bucks?" And the dog started to growl. Dave said, "No, no, it's me, Wilkes. I need you at the club."

Richie Havens was always around then. Richie was a funny guy. He would come in and play the hoots and the house managers would always tell him, "Look, come back tomorrow night. We'll put you on in front of the headliner. We'll pay you real money. A hundred bucks." Richie would say, "Fine." The next night, no Richie. The house managers would go out looking for him, and he'd be in Hank Washburn's basket house, up on stage, playing for nickels and dimes. They called it a basket house because they would pass around a basket after the performance to collect money for the artist, which was the performer's only pay.

Every Tuesday night was hoot night at the Bitter End, and those evenings form some of my fondest memories. There was no doubt that it was the bottom rung on the showbiz ladder. About an inch or two higher than oblivion. The audiences were usually receptive, and most performers flooded the pews with their faithful. Record labels and management companies used the club like crazy to audition acts or to pick up hot prospects. A singer might come up on stage with what might genuinely be termed a lame act, but for whatever reason this time the lameness would fade, the timing would actually work, the audience actually laughed when they were supposed to, and the hard-to-reach diminished chord would be reached just as the timbre in the voice cracks. A sensation would be born.

That was pretty much what happened when Kris Kristofferson introduced Stevie Goodman to New York audiences for the first time back in the early seventies. Kris actually pulled Stevie out of the audience and said, "This fellow's gonna sing you the best damn train song you ever heard." And Stevie went on to sing "City of New Orleans." Kris had one more ace up his sleeve. It was getting late and we had to clear the room for the next show, but Kris begged me to let him showcase one more act. I could never refuse Kris anything, so right after Stevie came off, Kris introduced John Prine. John went onstage and New York audiences heard "Sam Stone" for the first time. There were always a lot of agents from every record label in the room, but that night Jerry Wexler was in a side booth and signed John to Atlantic Records. What a lot of people don't know was that Harry and Tom Chapin were in the audience that night. When they found out that both Prine and Goodman came to New York via Chicago, Harry turned to Tom and said, "We got to go out to Chicago and find out what these guys are smoking."

Funnyman Jimmy Walker was really bad in the beginning, but he never gave up. There were usually a lot more singers than comics, and Jimmy got on more than he should have, which was very important to him. Jimmy would never take no for an answer, and he would try anything a hundred different ways until he succeeded in getting a laugh. He would drive me nuts. After bombing badly, he would run after me and say, "So how did you like the joke about the guy who gets stoned at the smorgasbord?" "It was stupid," I would say, "I thought it stunk." And Jimmy would say, "That's all right, but what about this one? This blind nun walks into a whorehouse by mistake and . . ." He would never quit.

You could often count on a surprise visit from practically anybody. Roger Miller would stop by because his brother worked in the kitchen. Sometimes he would get onstage, and other times he would take out his guitar in the kitchen and sing duets with his brother or one of the dishwashers. Neil Diamond, who was initially managed by Fred Weintraub, would come by to test new material. After he turned into a Las Vegas act, it's odd to think of Neil walking into the club in jeans and a corduroy work shirt, sitting on a barstool singing "Kentucky Woman" on his acoustic. Very often Odetta or Theodore Bikel might stop in for coffee and let themselves be coaxed onstage for a short set. Occasionally we would have to bring someone in because there just wouldn't be any talent for a hundred miles, and even as late as 1968, two dollars and fifty cents was nothing to sneeze at. When they pay to get in, you have to give them something. One night we brought in Bobby Hebb, who did about forty minutes, including his hit "Sunny."

Often a duo like the Sanjac of Novipazar will be funny and spirited, but deep in your heart you just know that two guys with a washboard and a guitar are probably not going to skyrocket. Long-forgotten names like the Hamilton Face or Common Ground or the Linksters tried hard to leave a lasting impression, but unlike the footprints outside Grauman's Chinese Theater, the footprints of most of these performers were imprinted in sand instead of concrete. But then the next act up might be two girls calling themselves the Simon Sisters, and they were just too magical to forget. Even though Lucy would occasionally sing off-key and Carly was almost always a nervous wreck, there was something about them.

Paul Simon and Art Garfunkel played the hoots for a long time. I think they had one suit between them. One wore the jacket and the other wore the pants. A lot of acts did that. They had a gray-haired manager named Walter who worked his ass off, but for the longest time they couldn't even get arrested. No one was buying them or their records. And this was when they were singing "The Sound of Silence." It was a very frustrating time. Once Simon and Garfunkel were playing, and there were people talking in the audience. Paul stopped playing and glared into the crowd and said, "The name of the game is to *listen!*"

For about a year the club ran a segment called the midnight drop-in. When we couldn't squeeze any more performances out of the regulars, it would often be midnight, which was still early. We decided to spread the word and see if anybody decent needed some time to work out new material. Flip Wilson did some sets. Richie Pryor did some sets too. Richie would often hang out to watch Bill Cosby whenever Bill played the club. In the beginning Richie wanted to be Bill Cosby, before he found his own voice. Anyway, Dick Reicheg was put in charge of running the midnight drop-ins. Dick ran into David Frye on the street one day. David was a great impressionist who didn't have much of a sense of humor. What he had was a lot of good writers. Dick said, "Hey, David, we're having a midnight hoot at the Bitter End. Do you want to come down?" "That's great," said David. "I got a lot of new material I want to try out. But I want to go on right away. What time does it start?" "The midnight drop-in?" said Dick. "It starts at midnight." "Okay, I'll be there." David Frye shows up, does his bit, and everything is great. The next day Frye runs into Dick again. "Are you guys doing that midnight drop-in thing again?" "Yeah, do you want to do a set?" "Sure, what time should I be there?" "Dave, it's a *midnight* drop-in. Come at midnight." So he comes, and again it's a nice night. The next day Frye runs into Dick again, and again they go through the same dialogue. "So what time should I come to this midnight drop-in?" "Why don't you come around 2:00 A.M.," said Dick, because now he's getting aggravated. It was like, who's buried in Grant's Tomb? Frye showed up at 2:00 A.M., and he was so mad he never came back.

We covered every possibility at the hoots. We even did an impromptu poetry reading with Muhammad Ali in 1963. Ali, or Cassius Clay, as he was calling himself then, was fighting Doug James at the Garden. All the New York newspapers were on strike. In order to drum up publicity, he came down to the club to read some of his poetry. It was not like he had composed *Paradise Lost*. He read the kind of doggerel that he used to chant in the ring to goad his opponents. It was a goof, but it got him the publicity he was craving. Even before he got to the club, there was a great scene as he proudly strode down Bleecker Street. He was dressed to kill, with a wry smile for the cameras, surrounded by his own entourage and hundreds of people following in his wake. He stood about a foot higher than anyone around him. It was a real happening.

Everything was going great until 1963, when ABC decided to give folk music a try. No one could deny its influence. The Kingston Trio and Peter, Paul and Mary were monster acts by now, filling spaces like Carnegie Hall. Joan Baez made the cover of *Time* magazine. Allan Sherman was making millions selling albums that spoofed the folk classics, and in that same vein, the Smothers Brothers were making hit records. Even groups like the Animals and the Beatles were doing songs like "House of the

Rising Sun" and "Taste of Honey." After years of pleading by people like Pete Seeger and Alan Lomax, the networks were going to try folk music on prime time. The show was going to be called *Hootenanny*.

ABC knew very little about folk music, and Procter and Gamble, the show's sponsors, knew even less. They all wanted to chase after this cyclone that was sweeping across America. But they didn't have a clue. All they knew was that folk music was big. The producers who created the format and aesthetics of the show were, in a demented way, very modern. They almost seemed to anticipate Beatlemania.

The shows were all taped at college campuses, and the kids were encouraged to scream. Somebody hired Jack Linkletter to moderate the show, which was like getting Pat Boone to emcee a rhythm and blues concert. The camera work was very fast and jumped from one set or location to another every two or three seconds. There were a number of stages so you could finish with an act and immediately introduce another without taking a breath. And always the audience screaming on cue. If you had Frank Sinatra up there or, indeed, the Beatles, it might have seemed believable, but it just didn't work with Boxcar Willie.

As far as the music went, ABC and the moneymen were even more in the dark than I was when I first took over the club. I might have thought Simon and Garfunkel was a drugstore, but these guys were far worse than me. What they needed was somebody on the inside who could act as adviser to the producer. So ABC hired Fred Weintraub without credit to act as talent spotter. On the surface it was perfect. The Bitter End was the greenhouse for all these young singers to grow and flourish. It was a natural to use the club as a conveyor belt to television and stardom. Fred would send the acts to the Ashley Talent Agency, and they would approve them for use on *Hootenanny*.

There was just one problem: Pete Seeger.

Fred was good friends with Pete and his manager, Harold Leventhal, and was in constant contact with him over Pete. Right from the start, you could tell that people were dragging their feet and stalling. Nat Hentoff broke the story in the *Village Voice* that Pete was being blacklisted. ABC said there was no blacklist. Then they blamed it on the sponsors. Then they claimed that Pete wasn't popular enough for national television. They were either spinning lies or insults. Here's the man who invented the very name for the damned show, and he couldn't get on. Fred was in the middle. He was getting the runaround and giving it to Harold. Finally a lot of people got very angry.

A group of performers got together and bought full-page ads in all the papers denouncing the blacklisting. There was a big meeting in Harold Leventhal's office where Joan Baez, Peter, Paul and Mary, Ed McCurdy, Dave Van Ronk, and Bob Dylan decided to boycott the show. Curiously, Pete's position was actually quite rational. He was hopping mad about the censorship but insisted that a boycott would be futile and bad. The *Hootenanny* show was good for folk music, like it or not, and the best thing to do would be to support it and eventually the blacklisting would break down. The boycott went into effect, but some performers ignored it. Theo Bikel thought it was stupid. Josh White and Maybelle Carter weren't about to bypass the dream of getting on a national TV show. Joan Baez said that she could forgive Maybelle Carter, but God help you if you are young and white and Jewish and want to make a splash. There was a line drawn in the sand.

The *Hootenanny* show split the folk community right down the middle. Peter, Paul and Mary apparently gave up a ten-thousand-dollar offer. Judy Collins appeared a number of times, but she had already signed contracts before she found out what they were doing to Pete. Tommy Makem refused to appear, but the Clancy Brothers went on. A lot of people told me that Ramblin' Jack Elliott would have probably helped his career immensely by appearing on the show. He refused. The Smothers Brothers became household names, and so did the New Christy Minstrels. The show was often lousy, but it did bring folk music to about fifteen million people who had never really heard it before. Pete was right in wanting to keep the show alive. His more idealistic protégés were perfectly happy with a face without a nose.

The word leaked out on campuses all over the country. Everywhere that the *Hootenanny* flatbed truck appeared with the ebullient Christy Minstrels and the grinning nerd, Jack Linkletter, there were sizable protests. It was getting embarrassing for ABC. There wasn't a single network show that would have hired Pete Seeger for anything, but ABC had put their foot in it by lying and then trying to explain away the lies by doubting Pete's professionalism and talent. The problem was never Pete's failure as a performer. Pete was feared because he was controversial, honest, and effective.

In the midst of all this hubbub some good things did happen. The Tarriers were first blacklisted and then, because of the protests, allowed to appear. America got a chance to see one of the first interracial singing groups. Not a small achievement. The Tarriers were actually scheduled to play the Bitter End the night of the taping, and so they had to find someone to fill in on short notice. Of course they asked Pete Seeger.

The boycott stayed in place and *Hootenanny*, because of its own stupidity and also because it no longer had the talent pool it thought it might have, rolled over and died at the end of the season. Because of the exposure they received, the Smothers Brothers went on to national fame and eventually went on CBS with their own variety show. The show became infamous for its constant fights with the censors and sponsors. One of the sponsors was Procter and Gamble. The ironic thing was that in 1965, on the *Smothers Brothers Comedy Hour*, only two years after *Hootenanny*, Pete Seeger finally appeared.

There are still people who hold a grudge against Fred and, by extension, the Bitter End for the *Hootenanny* affair. It's all childish. First of all, Pete and Harold never held a grudge. They still came by the club, Harold still booked acts into the club, and everybody was on speaking terms with everybody else. The next year, 1964, Ronnie Gilbert of the Weavers was practically in residence through the spring, summer, and fall. If anybody would have resented the club, it would have been an ex-Weaver, but there was no such animosity. Harold Leventhal called me in February 2000 to ask me if I could book Arlo Guthrie's daughter for a showcase. And Arlo played for me on any number of occasions and even recorded a live album.

After Woodstock came and went, there was a movie released by Columbia Pictures a few years later. Performers like Richie Havens, John Sebastian, Joni Mitchell, and Neil Young, whom I played at the Bitter End as unknowns, went on to achieve astonishing success. Even the announcers like Wavy Gravy and Chip Monck were old Bitter End hands. What many people don't realize is that the creative team who brought Woodstock to the screen included Fred Weintraub and Ted Ashley, formerly of the Ashley Talent Agency. I don't remember Joan Baez calling for a boycott of *Woodstock* because the producers were connected with the *Hootenanny* show. But then the movie was a huge success, and the album sold like crazy.

5

Woody, Coz, and Cavett

I don't want to achieve immortality through
my work. I want to achieve it by not dying.
                    —**Woody Allen**

ALL OF THE COFFEEHOUSES and most of the jazz clubs in Greenwich Village were known for their consistent presentation of great comics as well as for their musical bills. The jazz clubs followed a burlesque-hall blueprint and usually had comics to open their shows and warm up the audience. The coffeehouses just followed the pattern, especially when folk music replaced poetry as the wellspring of entertainment. Folk music benefited enormously from comic relief because folk music had a tendency to be solemn and redundant. For every Phil Ochs or Bob Dylan, there were a dozen traditional singers who reverently sang the same old standards. And, as I was quoted once, there were just so many times an audience could listen to Michael rowing his fucking boat ashore. There were many brilliant and revelatory moments when a folk music concert passionately burned with a great inner light. Sometimes it was like going to a union rally; sometimes it felt like going to church and listening to a boring sermon. Not all the time, but sometimes.

In the early sixties, something magical happened that could not have been predicted—that in four or five square blocks people like Woody Allen, Bill Cosby, Richie Pryor, Joan Rivers, Dick Cavett, and a couple of dozen less known but equally unique, funny people would all be trying to start a career. These were daring and singular talents. Just about anybody could pick up a guitar, learn a few chords, and get by as a folksinger. But you really needed to know what you were doing in order to get up on stage and deliver even ten minutes of comedic dynamite.

When Woody Allen first came to the Bitter End, he was already a pretty respected comedy writer. In fact, in the late fifties he had earned an Emmy nomination for his writing. Sid Caesar and Jack Paar were performing his gags on television, and there was good money in it. Milt Kamen introduced Woody to Sid Caesar while Caesar was meeting with Larry Gelbart, one of his most brilliant writers. Kamen said, "Sid, I want you to meet the young Larry Gelbart." Gelbart, understandably put out and only in his forties, said, "Excuse me, but *I'm* the young Larry Gelbart." Woody was married to a brainy girl named Harlene who was convinced he could become the next Molière. Woody's good friend and fellow comic, Len Maxwell, felt Woody should be doing his own stuff and suggested, besides a psychiatrist, that he see Jack Rollins and Charlie Joffe, who were making a name for themselves by managing acts like Harry Belafonte and Mike Nichols and Elaine May. When Woody first approached Rollins and Joffe, he resisted the notion of performing himself and expressed an interest in writing material for Nichols and May, who were the most sophisticated comedy act at the time. Jack Rollins said that Mike and Elaine wrote their own stuff. This would have been around 1961. Jane Rollins remembers the time because the Rollinses' daughter, Francesca, was a baby and just starting to crawl.

"Woody was sitting on the couch," said Jane, "and Francesca crawled up to him and pulled herself up by Woody's pants leg. And Woody knocked her down. She pulled herself up again, and he knocked her down again. Well, they became bosom buddies. When Woody's first album came out a few years later, the one with just his picture on the cover, Francesca was just starting to talk. She would point to the picture and say, 'Woood Dee.' Not 'Dada' or 'Mama,' but 'Woood Dee.'"

Woody eventually asked Jack to look at his own stuff, and Jack and Charlie fell over their feet laughing. They weren't sure what to do with Woody, but they agreed they would try to do something. They put him into a few nonpaying basement clubs to get his feet wet. Woody was just terrible. His material was great, but nobody in the audience seemed to care. And then Jack remembered the Bitter End.

Woody's first booking at the Bitter End was in early 1962. Woody was so nervous about performing that once Jack and Charlie actually had to stop him from trying to crawl out the back window of the club just before a performance. The problem was that Woody had no stagecraft in the beginning. He couldn't deliver his material. He recited it. Jack and Charlie would be in the back seats falling on the floor laughing, but it took a while for the audience and Woody to meet halfway. In what would become a pattern, Woody would perform his act, and Jack, Charlie, and Woody would then walk around Washington Square discussing how his performance could be improved, walk back to the Bitter End, and do the same thing over and over again. Woody played the club this way for years, sometimes for four- and six-month stretches, and either Jack or Charlie was at every show.

In the beginning Woody was a nervous wreck. When he came onstage, the audience didn't know who this guy was. There was no association with him. Nobody loved him. But his material was so incredibly good that he usually had the audience after the first couple of minutes. He had them locked. He was simply the best comedy writer. He always had killer material.

The anxiety and stress of performing was taking a toll on him physically and was also affecting his marriage. His wife, Harlene, would call up Jack in the middle of the night saying, "What are you trying to do to my husband? You're killing him. My husband is a shy and brilliant man. He could be a great writer, and you're turning him into a clown." It was upsetting for everybody. But Woody refused to capitulate, although many times he was close to quitting. "Let's give it another six months," someone would always say, and eventually Woody prevailed.

One of Woody's opening acts was a mime troupe run by Richmond Shepard, considered by many to be the best mime working in America, although as Richmond always maintained, "Mime is the only thing that pays less than poetry." Like the family that prays together, Richmond and his troupe were students of Sabud, which is a kind of spiritual exercise. They noticed that Woody was often a nervous wreck before he went onstage, so one day Richmond took Woody aside and told him about Sabud and how it worked, and Woody sat down on the floor and began to listen. Then he started to slowly breathe in and out with Richmond and the other mimes as they drew on this spiritual force they tapped, letting it run through them. Woody became very serene, and he started to smile and quiet down, and he calmly and peacefully walked out onstage and proceeded to bomb! It was one of the worst shows he ever did. He must have needed that tension to make his act work. He didn't talk to Richmond for about three weeks.

In the beginning of his career Woody was often an opening act. One group he opened for was a popular folksinging group called the Tarriers. The four-man group featured Eric Weissberg on guitar and banjo, who would eventually help create the soundtrack for the movie *Deliverance,* and Marshall Brickman on bass. Marshall would often sit in the back of the club listening as Woody performed. "Woody was like some exotic jungle bird that somebody had brought back from deepest . . . somewhere . . . with this amazing plumage," said Marshall. "It was like finding a brilliant new book by an author that no one ever heard of before."

Because he could tune his instrument faster than the other guys, Marshall was the one who did the talking for the Tarriers. Marshall was pretty comfortable onstage and actually started doing jokes and routines. It was during one insane six-month run at the Bitter End that Marshall and Woody began to collaborate. This partnership not only enhanced Woody's stand-up act but also, over the years, gave birth to numerous screenplays, of which four would eventually be filmed. One of them, *Annie Hall,* would win Woody and Marshall an Academy Award for best screenplay. By the end of that six-month run, incidentally, the Tarriers were opening for Woody.

In the very beginning, Woody often did not do well with the audience because his material was so new. It was an entirely new approach to comedy. He was still finding himself. Marshall was also trying to find himself. In the very beginning, Woody was doing a lot of "what if" premises. It wasn't all that personal yet. Like, "What if the Russians accidentally launched an ICB missile and it was going to hit New York and Khrushchev had to call Mayor Lindsay? What would the phone call sound like?" And then Woody would do Mayor Lindsay on the phone. But he was still lost. He was finding himself as a performer.

Then slowly he began to work in this spectacular, amazing new stuff, very intimate bits about his wife, psychoanalysis. It was all so audacious at that time. It was initially difficult for the audience to latch on to because Woody was really inside. He was so inside that it wasn't always good. People didn't talk about that stuff in public, much less try to get jokes out of it. Most comics were still doing mother-in-law jokes and routines about the suburbs and crabgrass.

The Tarriers were also managed by Rollins and Joffe, and it was actually Charlie Joffe who suggested that Marshall and Woody work together. It was not a chummy or particularly friendly or intimate arrangement. They didn't tell each other their troubles. It was rather a Gilbert and Sullivan relationship. Or maybe Gilbert and Gilbert. It was a little stiff, but they were both young and kind of shy. The relationship lasted for years. Even when Marshall became head writer for the *Tonight Show with Johnny Carson* and, later on, producer for the *Dick Cavett Show,* Woody and he would still get together and write. They wrote *Sleeper* while Marshall was on the Cavett show and Woody was on Broadway in *Play It Again, Sam.* Marshall worked every day from nine in the morning until about eight at night when the Cavett show was finished taping for the day. Woody had an eight o'clock curtain and wasn't finished until after eleven, but they would still meet for a couple of hours and work. Maybe that was how they came up with the title *Sleeper,* because they couldn't have gotten that much shut-eye.

Woody and the Bitter End were a perfect marriage. Like most performers whether they were singers, poets, or clowns, Woody and his managers used the club as a training camp or graduate school of performing. All the bugs and speed bumps in a particular bit could be honed and fine-tuned to perfection. Woody could bring the house down with lines like, "I got caught cheating on my metaphysics exam the other day. My professor claimed I was looking into the soul of the guy next to me." He had a wonderful bit about a library detective in search of unreturned books that was later reworked and dramatized by the *Seinfeld* writers for one of their shows. He could update spouse jokes with a vengeance as his career began to erode his first marriage. Woody would pull a snapshot out of his pocket and hold it up to the audience. "This is a picture of my wife in front of our new house," he would say. "My wife is the one with the shingles."

Hamilton Camp, Bob Gibson's onetime partner, remembers opening for Woody. "It was a horror. It was after I split up with Bobby Gibson, and I was broke in the Village and the tuner on my guitar was broke. I had to pull out a wrench after every song to readjust the pitch. One thing I noticed about Woody. I'd be standing backstage watching his act, and then when he was through, he would go in the back and keep his hands tight over his ears so he wouldn't hear the applause." At one point Jake Holmes, another comedian and singer-songwriter, was watching Woody after a gig, and Woody walked into the back room cupping and banging his hands over his ears and in the voice of a yenta kept saying, "He's bombing. . . . They don't like him. . . . They don't want him. . . . They hate him. . . . What is he going to do?"

During the early sixties the best bookings at the club were Woody Allen and another young and up-and-coming comic, Bill Cosby. With Bill or Woody headlining, we could often squeeze in four or five shows a night. They proved to be absolutely incredible for business and topped all the other performers, including the great folk acts.

Woody and Coz were completely different acts. Their stage personas were directly opposite ends of the spectrum. Coz would come on, and the audience just sat back, smiled, and said, "Ahhh." Everybody loved Bill immediately. I don't even remember what Cosby did. He was working on the Noah routine back then. Bill's first album, *Bill Cosby Is a Very Funny Fellow, Right?* is filled with all the material he created and worked out at the club at that time. In fact, it was recorded live at the Bitter End. He smiled and people loved him. Woody's material was often better than Bill's, but Coz was the better performer at the time. Woody hated performing, and the Bitter End waitresses used to kill him. When Bill Deseta was managing the club, he would get a bunch of girls in the kitchen, line them up in skimpy outfits, and send them out onstage to hug and kiss Woody because it would just destroy him. Most of the comics who played the club could improvise. Bill Cosby and Bobby Klein were great improvisers, but Woody did an act and he never varied one comma from that act.

Richie Pryor would stop in often to watch either Coz or Woody. Woody even told Richie once that if he wanted to be a comic, "Just watch me." This was a little later in his career, say, around 1964, when he actually started looking at the audience instead of fixating on the microphone. But Richie wasn't interested in Woody. Richie wanted to be the next Bill Cosby. Richie tried to do the Cosby style of comedy, but it didn't work, it didn't ring true. While Bill was always very funny, his material was very homey. Coz studiously stayed away from the race jokes he was doing when he first hit the Village. He excised that material completely from his act.

He was doing a lot of vignettes from childhood, like "Little tiny hairs growing out of my face." Roy Silver and Fred Weintraub were managing him in a kind of combined arrangement. Fred's idea was to make sure that Bill never said anything about race. It was not part of his act. They felt that they wanted to break him as a comic, not a black comic. The idea was to give him a broader base and consequently a larger audience. In a sense, it was a very liberal thing to do. A lot of people thought of Weintraub as a kind of liberal philistine, but his racial understanding was very good. He had a good handle on that. It was an astute thing to do, and in a quiet way, I think, it helped race relations by allowing Bill to be a comic who was acceptable to both the white and the black. It bridged a gap that needed to be bridged, because at the time there were people like Dick Gregory, who was something of a model, and he was wonderful, but he was a strident black voice. There certainly should have been strident black voices, but there also should have been one guy who wasn't, and I think that's what Bill did very well. It was a very important issue at that time. It eventually allowed Richie Pryor to become even more strident. So while in the beginning Richie's material was weak and disjointed a lot of the time, it also had an edge to it when it worked, and bit by bit it began to work more than fail. To a lot of people's taste, Richie was the funnier comic, but that was simply for preference. They were perfectly balanced and right for the times. By the end of 1964 Woody, Coz, and Pryor were skyrocketing.

As Woody and Coz began to hit television and the bigger nightclub venues, the second wave of comics began to come in. Dick Cavett came in 1964, stayed for six months, and bombed for six months straight. Audiences hated him with a passion. I mean with a passion. It wasn't even neutral hatred. It was like they wanted to kill him. He was very offensive onstage, and he just couldn't help coming off with a snotty, Yalie, "I'm better than you are, you fuckin' imbeciles" gloss. You could see the sneer all the way across the room. It never ebbed. He did six months of dead silence in the middle spot, and he killed everybody else because the headliners had to follow him. Dave Van Ronk once told me that if you followed Bill Cosby, you had a free fifteen minutes. Cosby made everyone feel so good that even if you stunk or were drunk and couldn't sing, the audience wouldn't catch on for a good fifteen minutes. But Cavett was just the opposite. To be fair to Dick, some people liked him. But no one left the club really laughing. But then some people don't mind spending an evening where they simply smile a lot.

The first night he performed at the Bitter End, he asked the announcer to tell the audience that a nice young man was going to come out and talk to them. It was downhill from there. Petrified, Cavett actually called up Woody to ask him for advice. Now when Woody first started performing, the Bitter End audiovisual man, Jon Gibbs, was bored one night, and instead of the usual introduction Jon said, "And now, direct from Bellevue insane asylum, Woody Allen." Woody walked out and gave Gibbs such a stare he actually started to worry that it might affect his job. After the show Woody said, "That's good, but from now on I'll write the intros."

When Woody found out what Cavett had used for his intro, he said, "Dick, the first thing you have to tell the audience is that you are a comedian and you are going to make them laugh." He also told Cavett to get back onstage right away. After this quick course in stagecraft, Cavett survived the next six months, but stand-up was definitely not his thing. I don't even think he wanted to really be a stand-up. Like many people—Joan Rivers is another example—Dick really wanted to be an actor. For whatever reason, and Woody may have influenced him, he tried to do a stand-up act. It wasn't that the act was bad. You just needed a master's degree to get half the jokes. David Brenner told me that all comedians have a "She's so ugly" joke. Woody's, for instance, involved cold gefilte fish on a plate. David's joke was that for Halloween, this girl didn't wear a mask, she just had a rubber band go from ear to ear around the back of her head. Well, Dick's involved a Picasso painting, in a cubist style that, like a jigsaw puzzle, falls to pieces. By the time the audience figured it out, Dick was already two jokes ahead. One line that usually worked involved a landlord who used immigrants so badly that he would sell them their own mail. He also did an impersonation of Richard Loo, a Hollywood Oriental character actor from the old days. It was a stretch.

Cavett has admitted that whenever he wakes up in a cold sweat, he is reliving his debut at the Bitter End. Marshall Brickman of the Tarriers had a great line about a fellow performing somewhere and "a bead of sweat came down his forehead, thereby obscuring it." That was Dick's first night.

He eventually found his niche by becoming one of the best interviewers on television. His shows were always miles ahead of Johnny Carson and Joey Bishop and the rest just because of the lineup of guests. Groucho Marx, Marlon Brando, Katharine Hepburn, Ingmar Bergman were huge and interesting artists who simply never did that kind of intimate television until Cavett charmed them. Who knows how he did it, but it worked.

There was always a pack of journeyman comics around. One of the first to ever play the club was Len Maxwell. It was Len who introduced Woody Allen to Rollins and Joffe. Len and Woody worked together up at a Pocono resort hotel called Tamiment. In the fifties Tamiment actually ran a staff of writers, actors and actresses, set designers, musicians, etc., and they would put on original variety shows. Len was a Woody disciple. Len said that once he felt, for whatever reason, that he wasn't funny. He couldn't figure out why. So he began to work on his appearance. He decided that he would wear a bow tie, and all of a sudden he was funny. He had some really good material. He was a clever writer, but he was always in the shadow of Woody. Len's real strength was in voices. Woody used him in *What's Up, Tiger Lily?* It was one of Woody's first film ventures, and he hated the whole idea. *Tiger Lily* was actually a bad, Japanese gangster movie, and Woody was hired to write a new script for it. He didn't want to do it, but Jack Rollins and Charlie Joffe insisted on it. They felt that if Woody had a writing credit to his name, it would be easier to promote him. So Woody wrote a hilarious script about a gang of thieves that abscond with a secret egg-roll recipe. He used actors and comics and singers like the Lovin' Spoonful, whom he knew from the clubs in the Village. There is a very funny trailer in the beginning of the film with Woody and Len. Len Maxwell did most of the crazier voices in the movie.

Len wound up suffering from a rare illness that left him paralyzed and confined to a wheelchair, but according to Len, "It's not that bad because I never liked walking." Len gained fame throughout the last thirty years by being the voice for Hawaiian Punch. "How'd you like a nice Hawaiian Punch?" Then the cartoon kid slugs the guy. One of his more memorable jokes was, "Do you know why prisoners can't escape from minimum-security jails? Because they have no walls to lean their ladders against." I always thought that was a very Zen, Woody Allen kind of joke.

Almost from the beginning of the Bitter End, Jake Holmes was hanging out. He first came to the Village from Long Island and joined in the hoots and the sing-alongs in Washington Square Park. He and his wife, Kay, were classically trained in opera. Jake and Kay came to the club as an act sometime in 1962. They used their middle names for some reason and called themselves Allen and Grier. They were very funny. Jake wrote most of the songs, and, rather than do stand-up, Allen and Grier did parodies of folk songs. They did songs like "Teenage Mother,"

"It's Better to Be Rich than Ethnic," and "Counterman," which was a chain-gang song relocated in a Chock Full O'Nuts restaurant. Pete Seeger reviewed them in his magazine *Sing Out!* and referred to them as "the most tasteless folk act I have ever seen." They were putting on folk music.

Allen and Grier recorded an album and wound up being run by Fred and Roy Silver. When Jake eventually had to go in the army, Roy, splendid fellow that he was, stole Jake's wife, and that was the end of Allen and Grier. It was also, more or less, the end of Kay, for Roy treated her badly, and Roy would eventually have his own problems. But Jake survived rather well.

Jake was understandably upset about losing his wife, and Fred made Roy persona non gratis for a while. Fred always fancied himself another Albert Grossman. He saw Albert moving people around, hooking them up, and creating acts like Peter, Paul and Mary. Well, right around this time, there were two out-of-work actors named Jim Cannell and Joan Rivers. Fred felt bad for Jake and saw an opportunity to create another act like the Revuers, which is how Betty Comden, Adolph Green, and Judy Holliday got started. He put Joan and Jim together with Jake and called them Jim, Jake and Joan, and they were unique, to say the least. Jim could sing a little but he wasn't funny, Joan was funny but she couldn't sing, and Jake could do both. Jim and Joan hated each other and would try to kill each other in between sets. They would always turn to Jake to be the mediator, but Jake would have none of it.

For about a year they played the Bitter End almost every other week. And the reviews were not that bad, even if no one was particularly interested in taking them on full-time. They survived for a year. The amazing thing is not that they lasted as long as they did artistically but that they didn't kill each other. Joan went on to become Joan Rivers, whatever that means these days. Jim Cannell acts in Hollywood, and someone swore they saw him in the Larry Flynt movie. Jake went on to become the most successful jingle writer in New York. He made a killing writing stuff like "I'm a Pepper, You're a Pepper" for Coca-Cola and "Be . . . All That You Can Be" for the U.S. Army.

Very often there were special comedy nights, and the audience would be saturated with fans and other comics. One night Dick Shawn played a minimarathon, and during the set he recognized a very funny comic-mimic named Will Jordan. When he took the stage, he called attention to Will, pointing him out in the crowd and calling him one of the funniest men in show business. Then Larry Storch, who became a hit on TV's *F Troop*, came onstage and did the same thing. "I just want to point out my good friend Will Jordan, one of the funniest guys," and made him stand up and take a bow. A forgotten, third comic came on and said, "I don't know who the hell Will Jordan is, but if he's that funny, what is he doing down there?"

There were other comics like Adam Keefe, Howie Storm, and George Hopkins who held down the fort and were actually very funny. Adam Keefe was a very tall, cadaverous solo who would walk out onstage, glare at the audience, and say, "They're tearing up the street in front of my building—again." That image was so funny to New Yorkers that it always got a laugh. But then the bit wouldn't go anywhere, and he'd be off on something else. He could never quite work a beginning, middle, and end into his performances. Adam's best bit was an imitation of a movie that has been badly edited or spliced back together, and so as the film would run, there would be crazy skips and segues and leaps. It was hilarious, and Adam did all the voices and sound effects right down to the racket the projector would make as the film ran around the spindles. Then it was on to something else.

Many people considered George Hopkins the funniest

comedian they ever saw. I think George was the guy who would occasionally make his entrance onstage by driving in the front door on a motorcycle. The problem with George was that, when he was at his best, nobody in the entertainment business would show up. They were going to skip that night or there was another show to see somewhere else. And when agents, managers, and record producers were in the club, George would get bumped or he'd show up half in the bag, and for some reason he never succeeded the way he probably should have. I think he is still working on cruises and the occasional nightclub engagement.

Howie Storm went on to work with Woody Allen in some of the early movies and eventually became a distinguished director in television. Probably one of the saddest stories is Vaughn Meader. Vaughn Meader was not an original. He was the most famous imitation. He could do Jack Kennedy better than Jack Kennedy, and he made an album in 1962 that was bought by everybody in the U.S., including the Kennedys. It was called *The First Family*. The material was great, and he was as hot as Elvis until November 1963. After Kennedy was assassinated, the American public never forgave Vaughn Meader and actually refused to give him a second hearing. I know he tried to make a comeback a number of times, but it just didn't work.

6

FOLK ROCK AND ITS INVENTORS

*There is nothing remarkable about it. All one
has to do is hit the right keys at the right
time and the instrument plays itself.*
—**J. S. Bach**

THROUGHOUT THE SIXTIES rock and roll blindsided the
music business. It just pushed every other musical form aside.
In the beginning, television and the established venues like
Carnegie Hall resisted rock. Few producers, sponsors, or impre-
sarios gave it more than a passing thought. The great fifties A&R
man for Columbia Records, Mitch Miller, once told Rosemary
Clooney, "Don't worry, rock and roll will be dead in six
months." Once these characters realized how much money there
was to make, the obstinacy quickly eroded. But there was also
a very interesting transitional period. The social and political
upheaval in the sixties kept folk music going strong. Folk music
has a redemptive, spiritual facet to it. And let's face it, most people turn to prayer when times are rough. For people out on the
streets and the protest lines, facing racist cops in Birmingham,

or being beaten and shot at by National Guardsmen, the great folk songs gave a voice to their anger, fear, and hopes. When Peter, Paul and Mary or Pete Seeger sang "Man of Constant Sorrow," there was an understanding that the pain expressed in that song was poignantly relevant to what was happening out on the streets and even to what was happening in Southeast Asia. The only problem was that, over time, most people weren't that interested in paying to hear folk music performed professionally anymore. They had heard it all before, and the songs were in their hearts.

The reason that the Bitter End is still in operation after nearly forty years is that we changed with the times. As early as 1963 but especially by 1964, after the Beatles came to America, folk music had to change or risk losing its young audience. It was steeped in tradition, which meant a lot of the songs were old and repetitious, and you couldn't dance to it. Simple as that. But folk songs were so much more interesting than "Louie Louie" or "Do-Wah Diddy." The logical thing to do was to take a folk song and rock it. That is what a group called the Big Three did exceptionally well. The Big Three was the house band of the Bitter End throughout 1963, and they had a big influence on people like John Sebastian, the Chapin Brothers, Jimi Hendrix, and others. Their music and the couple of albums they made came out about two years before anybody had thought up the term "folk rock." They were accidental folk rock.

The Big Three were Jim Hendricks (not Jimi Hendrix), Tim Rose, and Cass Elliot. Cass Elliot would join up with John Phillips and his merry band to form the Mamas and the Papas about two years later. Jimi Hendrix (not Jim Hendricks), ironically, would wind up playing across the street at the Café Au Go Go, as Jimmy James and the Blue Flames. He opened for John Hammond Jr., and all the guitar players in the Village, no matter where they were playing, would always try and sneak in to see one of "Jimmy's" sets. Jimmy, for some reason, couldn't break out in America, so he went to England and came back as the Jimi Hendrix Experience, and the rest was history, at least for a few more years.

Tim Rose was the real creative force behind the Big Three. He also played with Jake Holmes and with a band called the Thorns. Probably the best early example of folk rock was Tim Rose's arrangement of "Hey Joe." "Hey Joe" was a bouncy folk song, a slightly more upbeat "Tom Dooley." Well, Tim played it like a 6/8 blues and turned it into a passion play. Jimi Hendrix heard his arrangement and more or less copied it, note for note, for his first album.

Tim was one of the most exciting acts ever on the Bitter End stage. He was mesmerizing. He was also one of the most hostile guys you ever met in your life and pretty much killed his own career because he was so hostile to everybody. If he could have saved it all for the stage, he would have been a major star because he had a real raspy voice that would just tear your heart out. He had an intensity that didn't belong in folk music. He lives in England now, has mellowed a bit, and has a pretty good following over there. Cass was Tim's female counterpart, and together they could grab an audience by the throat. But the volatile nature of their personalities wasn't a good glue, and the band finally broke up. Cass and Tim Rose? You put them together in the same room, and eventually there had to be murder.

Another group that lays claim to being the first folk rockers was the Chapins. The Chapins included Tom, Steve, and sometimes Harry, and sometimes their dad, Jim, used to sit in. Jim Chapin was a big-band drummer from the thirties and forties and played with swingers like Glen Gray. He wrote the most influential jazz-drum instruction book I know of. In fact, after forty years, the Jim Chapin jazz drum method is still in print. The Chapins took the Big Three one step further. The Big Three did have some very lame material. For some reason, "Winkin', Blinkin', and Nod" got a lot of mileage. The Simon Sisters even recorded that, and the Simon Sisters were definitely not folk rock, although Carly turned out to be pretty funky later on. At one point, there was some talk of putting the Simon Sisters and the Chapin Brothers together as a kind of new New Christy Minstrels, but it never panned out.

The Chapins took over as house band after the Big Three went their separate ways. They played into the late sixties, until one day I got a call from an executive interested in starting production on a new children's television show called *Make a Wish*. The producers needed a singing, songwriting host. At first, they tried to get James Taylor, but James at that time was experimenting with a lot of different lifestyles and was unavailable. I was in the club when the call came through, and I recommended Tom. Tom Chapin went on to work for *Make a Wish* for years, writing and performing his own songs, using Harry's songs when he could, and winning Emmy and Peabody awards.

By 1964, the old guard was hanging tough, but it was clear that lines were being drawn in the sand. Fred wasn't really keen on rock and roll and kept holding on to the traditional acts. He played ex-Weaver Ronnie Gilbert for most of the summer of 1964. He also began creating groups like he had seen Albert Grossman do. Fred brought in the Serendipity Singers from Colorado and helped produce them. They were an imitation of the New Christy Minstrels and had a *Billboard* chart hit with "Crooked Little Man," which was just a rearrangement of the nursery rhyme "There Was a Crooked Man." The chorus was "Don't let the rain come down." When the Serendips were on the road, Fred had a backup group called the Bitter End Singers.

Although the audience for traditional folk music was dwindling, Fred still managed to fill the club because he was a hell of a promoter.

Fred Weintraub had always been a sophisticated publicist, and to keep all his many irons in the fire, he hired Mort Wax, a professional publicist, and a guy named Michael Goldstein to think up the unthinkable. Mike Goldstein was one of the greatest press agents in the Village. He had the Club Cheetah on the cover of *Life* magazine complete with full-color photos, full story, the works—two weeks before the club opened. Cheetah was the first big discotheque. Arthur's was around and so was the Peppermint Lounge, but they were small. Cheetah was an enormous room. It was the first of the monster clubs, and the modeling agencies used it a lot. It was more like Studio 54. And Goldstein represented Cheetah.

Mike Goldstein helped start the *East Village Other,* which was an alternative to the *Village Voice.* He used to come down to the club and figure out all kinds of weird promotional deals, and just about everybody thought he was nuts. He wanted to do Saturday morning shows for kids—free lollipops and prizes. There was always a love-hate relationship with Mike. Anyway, bit by bit, rock and roll was insinuating itself into every corner of America. The folk acts themselves were changing.

A good example of that was a group called the Modern Folk Quartet. They played the club around that time. One of the leaders of the group was Jerry Yester. They had a strong traditional folk act, and they were very good. When the group came to New York in 1963, the first parking space they found was in front of the Bitter End. Once when the Modern Folk Quartet was working the club, they found a canister of helium in the dressing room. We often did promotions and had to blow up hundreds of balloons. Well, Jerry and the group used to do this five-hundred-year-old Spanish madrigal called "Riu, Riu Chiu." They often used that song to open their shows because it was a very startling piece. This night they decided, for a laugh, that it would be a great idea if they all took a huge lungful of helium. The four of them started walking toward the stage, which was a long walk. They had to leave the dressing room carrying their instruments, walk through the crowd, and mount the stage. They soon realized that they had no oxygen in their lungs because of all the helium. They got a few feet from the stage and started to pass out. One by one, they began to stumble and in these high-pitched, dwarf voices said, "Ooooo, I don't think I can make it."

By 1966, the Modern Folk Quartet was slowly changing into a rock band. They would do a folk show and then close with some folk rock numbers. That's when they recruited John Sebastian as a drummer. John would be playing his own stuff at the Night Owl and then would run over, in between shows, and play for the Quartet. Ironically, a couple of years later Jerry Yester wound up joining the Lovin' Spoonful. Jerry told me that one of his great memories was around 1968 when he happened to be looking for Zal Yanovsky. He stuck his head in the door of the Bitter End and saw Bette Midler on stage. "I turned to the doorman," said Jerry, "and yelled, 'Who the hell is that?' She was doing 'Leader of the Pack.'"

The Modern Folk Quartet was managed by Herb Cohen, who also managed Judy Henske. Judy was a regular through most of 1963, '64. She was a tall, bluesy guitar player who sang in a very kick-ass style. Fred must have been crazy about her because he wound up casting her in an off-Broadway musical production called *Go Go Loves Me*. I forget who wrote the music, but the book was written by Anita Loos, and it was one of her few failures. It ran for one night. Fred produced and directed it, which may have been the problem.

Judy worked with Woody Allen a lot. Judy was a real intellect and read everything she could get her hands on. She read fiction, philosophy, drama, comedy, everything and anything. So did Woody, and they would often recommend books to each other or discuss what they read. When they were in different cities, they would often call each other for marathon telephone calls that sometimes lasted seven or eight hours. Woody very loosely patterned some of his characters after Judy. Judy was raised in the Midwest, and there is a famous scene in *Annie Hall* where Woody goes back to Annie's home for a visit and her family sees him as a rabbi. Well, he was imagining Judy's family in that scene.

I think folksinger David Buskin put it best about the tailspin that folk music was taking: "I fell in love with folk music, decided that that was what I wanted to play, and an hour and a half later folk music was dead." That wasn't quite true, but it was close enough. David Buskin now makes an excellent living writing music and lyrics for radio and television commercials and performing as New York's premier singer-songwriter wit. John Denver took over for Chad Mitchell in the Chad Mitchell Trio until, like many folk acts, it was made insignificant in the wake of rock's onslaught. John was all set to quit show business for good. He even made a final tape recording of a few of his songs for friends. Peter, Paul and Mary got hold of the tape and heard John's song "Leaving on a Jet Plane." They recorded it and made it a number-one record. That happy moment put John Denver back on the map and started him on his brilliant solo career. He kicked off one of his tours at the club back in 1971.

The most powerful thing in the Village then was the effect of the British Invasion and the eclipse of folk music as the number-one musical art form. I think that the Bitter End did something unique in that it allowed acts to make a smooth transition from folk to rock. It allowed people who were changing to go on play-ing. We had a very different policy than, say, the Troubadour out in California, which took a longer time doing that. Their policy was, "Hey, we're not folk anymore. You can't work here."

It was an amazing time. Almost overnight hordes of folk clubs transformed into little rock clubs. All the pawnshops were cleaned out of electric guitars. At least 75 percent of the people who started in folk music kind of changed from tadpoles to frogs and started making rock records and little demos. There was a lot of commiseration, a lot of people helping other people. If some-body got a record deal, you cheered for them. Very often, if you got a record deal, you would hire your friends to play backup on at least one or two tracks. At the time, it wasn't all that compet-itive. In that respect, the folk tradition was still alive.

Besides traditionalists like Ronnie Gilbert, the Bitter End hired the Womenfolk, who often were backed up by Spike Lee's dad, Bill, on bass. In spite of their name, the Womenfolk were great, funky singers. Jim McGuinn, who backed up the Chad Mitchell Trio, changed his name to Roger and helped found the Byrds. Although the press was calling it folk rock, the music coming out of the Village by the mid- and late sixties was slow-ly evolving into a form that refused to be categorized. Acts began to incorporate aspects of folk, rock and roll, the blues, jazz, and even classical music. That was probably the most amaz-ing aspect of it all. You could walk down Bleecker or MacDougal Street on any given night and see Tom Paxton at the Gaslight. Over at the Garrick Theater the Mothers of Invention would be rehearsing. The Lovin' Spoonful would be playing at the Night Owl. Jerry Jeff Walker or Joni Mitchell would be at the Bitter End, and Janis Fink, before she became Janis Ian, might be play-ing the Broadside Hoots at the Village Gate. Who was playing what kind of musical style? Who cared? It was all great.

Tim Hardin was a perfect example of a singer and song-writer who refused to be pigeonholed. Acts like Tim Hardin began to make their presence felt in a strong way. For some reason that I could never quite understand, a pitfall into drugs and booze seemed to go with the territory. Tim Hardin was a tragic example of that. Tim Hardin signed away his writing and music to keep himself in drugs. He wrote beautiful compositions like "If I Were a Carpenter" and "Misty Roses" that have now become standards not only in folk music but in the rock and roll and jazz world. He was so talented, but he had no control of his life. He used to stay with me at my home in Woodstock, but it would always turn into a tragedy when I found he had broken into my liquor closet and drunk himself into a stupor. Some guys are like puppies that break their leash and run headlong into traffic. There's no way you can stop them. Once I was hanging out with Dion and we were talking about music that we liked, and I told him one of the most beautiful songs I ever heard was "Reason to Believe." Dion said, "That's by Timmy Hardin. Oh my God, I love that song too." And he ran right out and bought the album.

Once when Tim played the Bitter End, Harry Chapin was in the audience. He came in specifically to hear Tim because, for a while, Tim Hardin was almost as big as Dylan, and he was a major influence on a lot of young songwriters, Harry included. Harry hadn't made it big yet, although he had played the club a number of times with his brothers. He was just one of a dozen or so fans in the audience. The show was bad because Tim was bad. The Bitter End is such an intimate club that you can see the tracks on a guy's arm from the back row. Harry never forgot that night. On one of Harry's subsequent albums, called *Short Stories*, he wrote a beautiful song called "Changes." The first verse poignantly describes what that evening was like, right down to the two-dollar soft drink, the feel and sound of the audience, and the inevitable tears to follow. Tim died later on out in California, broke, from a drug overdose.

Phil Ochs was another painful case. Phil came to the Village from the Midwest in the early sixties. Phil always seemed to me to have everything backwards. I think Phil wanted to be a rock and roll star first, but because of his guitar-playing ability, which was minimal, he got into folk music. Phil thought that you could change the world through political commitment. He also had problems that, if he could have held on a little bit longer, might have been diagnosed and cured through medication. I think Phil was a singer whose musical ideas translated perfectly into folk rock. If he could have only expanded his lyrical content to include a walk in the rain with the one you love every once in a while, he might have had a wider audience. Phil was loved by a small but devoted fan base. The extraordinary thing about Phil's fan base was that it included practically every musician, poet, political activist, artist, and singer on the planet. His albums rarely sold big. He was practically never on the radio, and yet more books and articles have been written about him than most of the noticeably bigger names.

Phil was funny and passionate, but too often his shows sounded like lectures. Musically a song like "Outside of a Small Circle of Friends" is the epitome of folk rock. But in the end, he wanted to be the second coming of Elvis. By the end of his career, and his life, Phil was making an almost sordid name for himself in the Village. He was in bad shape and wouldn't or couldn't help himself. I remember him always being surrounded by an entourage of hangers-on. I tried to get him to perform, but he would always make an excuse. He was running up bar tabs and refused to do anything about it. One day we had an argument over the bill, and Phil said, "I'll tell you what I'll do. We'll have a backgammon championship." At the time, Phil was very vain about his backgammon playing.

"I can't play backgammon, Phil," I said. He told me that I could choose a champion. We made stakes. If I lost, I was to supply him with a hotel room, lots of booze, and a hooker. If Phil lost, he would play the club, clean up his tab, and have some left over. I was hoping that if he got his ass back onstage and performed, he might get back on track. It would be a chance to perform any new material he had been working on. We actually drew up contracts.

There was a restaurant in New York called Knickers. It was known as a hangout for backgammon players, and I called the owner and asked him if he would play for me. His name was Mike Halverian. Phil knew all about Mike and agreed to the terms. They would play three games, and if Phil won just one of the games, he would win the bet. Phil arrived at the restaurant with his usual entourage of parasites, this time with a couple of big-breasted women in tow. He even arranged for TV cameras. Game one and Phil lost. He was half in the bag and getting very angry. The girls were there for a purpose. In case of a loss, Phil would get them to expose themselves and try to distract Mike. To their credit, they refused to go along with any of that nonsense. It was so pitiful that I went into the adjoining bar and had a drink. Game two and Phil lost. The third game was never finished. Midway through the game, Phil realized that he was going to lose. He kicked over the game board and left. He never honored the contract.

His behavior got to be so bad that I finally had to throw him out of the club. One evening Phil broke onto the stage of the Bitter End while Ramblin' Jack Elliott was in the middle of his set. Phil disrupted the show. I told him that he was never to come back to the club in a drunken condition. "If you're ever hungry,

I'll feed you. But no more booze."

I kept aware of Phil's comings and goings. Like the time my dishwasher came in to proudly tell me that he had just lent Phil a couple of bucks. I was so furious. Here was a dishwasher who Phil had scammed out of money by making the poor guy think he was important. Wow, he lent Phil Ochs money. One day Phil walked into the club. I hardly recognized him. He was disheveled, unwashed, a wreck. "Paul," he said, "you told me that if I was ever hungry you would feed me." "That's right, Phil," I said. "What would you like?" He told me he wanted a chicken salad sandwich. I had one of the waitresses bring him the sandwich. He finished it, thanked me, and left. It was the last time I saw him alive. A few weeks later he hanged himself in his sister's home out on Long Island.

At the funeral, I remember one of the leeches that used to follow him around, calling himself a friend, drinking and snorting up Phil's money. The guy actually had the nerve to come over to me and say, "What are you doing here? You weren't Phil's friend." I said, "You son of a bitch, I was his friend. I tried to get him to stop killing himself. It was parasites like you that helped kill him. If I ever see you in my club, I'll break your legs." After Phil's funeral there was a big memorial concert that was attended by a lot of people, fans, big names. The hangers-on never showed up. When the memorial service ended, we all went back to the Bitter End and partied long into the morning. We were all trying to remember the good times. On a wonderful Tom Paxton album called Heroes there is a song about Phil. Ironically, Tom had the same final, tragic image of Phil that I had. In one of the verses of the song, Tom sings, "The last time I saw you was outside the Other End." The song documented that time when I owned the club but had to rename it the Other End for a few years. The chorus was "Gone, gone, gone by your own hand."

I was slowly beginning to realize that the kids who were coming of age in the sixties and early seventies were unique in many subtle ways. And it involved more than just living through all the dramatic changes going on around them. There was a oneness that kids today don't seem to have. Maybe it was because they were baby boomers and there were so many of them. Maybe it was because they were positioned in time to be intimately knowledgeable about a very complex and hypocritical American past and an America that was changing irrevocably. They were the first generation that was raised on television, but there were only three channels. Everybody saw the same images, got the same news, and heard the same music. There were no computers, no Internet. There just weren't a million little cubbyholes to crawl into. I don't know how else to put it except to say that they began to absorb each other.

I always thought it was fascinating that East Coast kids like Elliot Charles Adnopoz and Ronald Clyde Crosby could grow up and become Ramblin' Jack Elliott and Jerry Jeff Walker respectively. Or that a midwestern Jewish kid like Bobby Zimmerman would want to grow up to be Woody Guthrie. Everybody was picking pieces of personalities and musical styles and making them their own. When the notion of making folk music rock really took hold, everybody brought their own special feel to it.

One of the best creators of the country style of folk rock was my good friend Mickey Newbury. Mickey came into town via Nashville with a string of songs that were destined to become hits. One of his first big ones was "I Just Dropped In to See What Condition My Condition Was In." One of the Bitter End's favorite performers back in the early sixties was Mike Settle. Mike was from Oklahoma and wrote beautiful melodies and lyrics. Like everyone else, he decided to abandon pure folk and formed the First Edition with an unknown lead singer named

Kenny Rogers. When their first album came out, most of the songs were written by Mike, but the big hit from the album was Mickey Newbury's 'I Just Dropped In. . . ."

Once when Mickey was playing the club, he did something he rarely did. He sang a song written by someone else. "You'll be hearin' from this guy soon," said Mickey. The song he sang was "Me and Bobby McGee." It was the first time anybody in New York ever heard it.

Sure enough, about six months later, as I was walking down Bleecker Street, Shel Silverstein came running up to me. "Paul," said Shel, "I want you to meet a guy that's going to be a big star." In my business, people are always coming up to you and saying those magic words. Usually they are agents or managers. But this was Shel. Shel Silverstein had been around since before the Flood. He was in the audience and heard Bob Gibson and Bob Camp play their legendary set at the original Gate of Horn in Chicago. It was recorded and became one of the most popular and enduring folk albums ever. Shel wrote the liner notes. He was a striking man, big, burly, and bald, with a domineering goatee, but gentle as a lamb. He was a rich talent. If you don't like his music, try looking at his drawings for *Playboy* magazine. If you don't like them, you'll probably love his books for children. Anyway, it was Shel who introduced me to Kris Kristofferson.

Kris was also big and burly, and, at the time, he looked pretty scruffy. We shook hands, and Shel insisted that I put him on that very night. I said, "Shel, I'll be happy to put him on if you play a set too." Shel wasn't into that, but he promised to come on and sing a song or two. Shel was a constant songwriter, but he rarely performed. In fact he had hired a band called Dr. Hook and the Medicine Show who did nothing else but perform Shel Silverstein songs.

When Kris hit the stage, it was one of the most wonderful moments I can recall. I knew that the songs that came out of him that night would endure. Not only did he do "Me and Bobby McGee" but also "For the Good Times," "Sunday Mornin', Comin' Down," "Help Me Make It through the Night." It was just magical. A few weeks later he was being written up in all the papers, and his original album, called *Kris Kristofferson,* was repackaged and reissued as *Me and Bobby McGee.* Kris and I would go on to become good friends.

When it was Shel Silverstein's turn to perform a few songs, he got up onstage and I couldn't get him off. He must have performed for over an hour.

As Kris's popularity grew, so did his generosity. It was Kris who brought John Prine and Stevie Goodman into the club and got them their record deals. Getting record deals is what the Bitter End has always been famous for. To show you how nuts it was back then, Carly Simon decided to go out on her own. The Simon Sisters made an album, but it never took off. Lucy got married and decided to concentrate on raising her kids. Carly wrote a dozen or so songs and made one of her first appearances as a solo at the Bitter End. Carly was always shy and suffered from terrible stage fright. I always admired her guts in somehow overcoming a fear that seemed likely to strangle her. Just before her opening-night performance, she was in her dressing room with Buzzy Linhart. Buz was a Village fixture and already established. His drummer used to date Bette Midler, so Bette saw Buzzy and his band a lot. One of Buzzy's best tunes was called "Friends," which Bette wound up using as her theme song. Anyway, Buzzy and Carly also used to date, and Buzzy came by to give her encouragement because he knew what terrible stage fright she had. While they were in the dressing room, Carly asked Buzzy to sing her something in order to calm her down. Buzzy stood behind her and massaged her neck while he sang sweetly to her. All of a sudden there comes a knock on the door, and a voice cries out, "Hey you in there singing. I'm a recording producer. Have you been signed by anyone?" For all the stage fright, Carly has been quoted as saying, "I'm most comfortable singing at the Bitter End."

While I was running the day-to-day operations at the club, Fred was beginning to really extend his empire. He had started a management company called Fredanna and began representing people. The Four Seasons, Jim, Jake and Joan, the Pickle Brothers, the Bitter End Singers, Neil Diamond, and a host of other acts were all managed out of the Bitter End. One of the sharpest ideas he had involved colleges and universities. Fred worked out a kind of NCAA operation to promote his acts. He organized a couple of hundred colleges, all over the country, to sponsor performers. Fred collected an initiation fee and then started shipping his acts out. The colleges would feed and house the performers, give them a stage and a couple of bucks, and send them off to the next gig. If you were in school during the late sixties and early seventies and saw people like Harry Chapin, Jerry Jeff Walker, Paul Siebel, or Jake Holmes, they most likely came your way via the Bitter End.

One of the oddest connections I remember uncovering via Fredanna was this. The Four Seasons were not really a Bitter End act. They were very pop oriented. The creative force behind the Four Seasons was not Frankie Valli but the keyboard player, Bob Gaudio, who wrote most of the hits. During one of the more bizarre stylistic metamorphoses, the Four Seasons decided to become relevant and recorded an album called *The Imitation Life Gazette*. It was written by Bob and Jake Holmes, whom I love, but the album was a complete bomb. Jake and Bob Gaudio didn't give up, however. They decided to try collaborating one more time. Now, the Four Seasons, and especially Frankie Valli, were big fans of my old boss, Frank Sinatra. Somehow Jake and Bob convinced Sinatra, who must have been looking to become relevant himself, to let them write a theme album for him. It was called *Watertown,* and it was one of Sinatra's worst albums. But that's the way the music business was back then. You have to remember that the *Billboard* charts were a conglomeration of every kind of singer and style imaginable. It wasn't like today when there are charts for every little genre and subgenre. I still remember looking at the *Billboard* charts in 1966 and watching Frank Sinatra's "Strangers in the Night" fight it out for the number-one record in the country with the Beatles's "Paperback Writer," only to have both of them wind up losing to Tommy James and the Shondells and his version of "Hanky Panky."

Van Morrison came to the Bitter End with Danny Armstrong and Charlie Brown. At that time my good friend Bert Berns was managing him. Bert had already made a name for himself by writing such rock and roll classics as "Twist and Shout" and "Hang on Sloopy." Anybody who has seen Van the Man over the years and thinks that he knows Van's style probably doesn't know the whole story. When Van played the club, it was about the time when the Who and the Yardbirds were around. It was during the time when bands were smashing up their instruments onstage.

Van had hired three black background singers from the Bronx to sing with him, and he was really wild. He was doing a song called "TB Sheets" that was part of his act at the time, and he got crazy. He started swinging the microphone around his head and the girls are trying to sing the chorus: "TB sheets ooooooo." And they're ducking as the microphone is flying over their heads. Van wouldn't let up and started kicking the microphone stand. The girls are singing and their faces are getting more and more wild as Van's getting more and more crazy. He finally kicked over the microphone stand. Then he started kicking over the front row of tables. Ice-cream sodas and Cokes started flying everywhere. Charlie and Danny kept right on playing; they couldn't care less. I think they were used to it. Van was completely off the wall, and these poor girls are ducking and hiding, and suddenly the three of them just walked offstage. Van kept right on singing, and about two minutes later, with their fur coats on, the girls walked right out the door. One of them turned to the other and said, "That motherfucker's crazy." Only a few people noticed what happened because everybody in the club was so nuts. Van recorded it on his *Blowin' Your Mind* album.

The smoothest transition from folk to rock came via people like Joni Mitchell, James Taylor, Neil Young, and Randy Newman. Neil Young actually opened for Joni Mitchell. We had to bill him as "Neil Young, formerly of the Buffalo Springfield" because nobody knew who he was. Joni was always hanging around the club because she had fallen in love with a songwriter named David Blue. David was a writer, singer, actor, and general crazy person. He was a kind of Bob Dylan clone. If Bob changed his hairstyle, then David would change his. If Bob wore a certain kind of shirt, then David would do likewise. I know he drove Joni nuts. He was constantly broke, and Joni was always lending him money. Somebody told me that her checkbook had more entries for David Blue than Bell Telephone or ConEd. Once he came pleading with her to lend him some money or he was going to be put out of his apartment. She had already sworn she would never lend him money again, but she finally relented. About an hour later she saw David walking down the street with candy and a dozen roses. He had cashed her check and was on his way to see a new girl.

David, like everybody else in the Village, used to hang out at the restaurant above the Bitter End called the Tin Angel. The Tin Angel was owned and operated by the Bitter End. When Joni finally recorded her first album, the last song on the second side was called "Tin Angel." It's a song about David. David played with Bob Dylan on a number of occasions, but his career never really took off. He died jogging in Washington Square Park in 1982. Joni Mitchell read the eulogy at his memorial service.

Randy Newman played the club occasionally. In the beginning I wasn't sure whether or not Randy would be a hit at the Bitter End. He was just starting out as a performer. Warner Brothers was promoting the hell out of him, and they made booking easy. If he bombed, they would pick up the tab. He never bombed. I never could figure out why Warners was so particularly hot for Randy Newman. Somebody finally told me. Randy Newman's dad was a successful dentist out in Texas, but his uncles were Lionel, Emil, and Alfred Newman, the most prolific and creative musicians on the Warner Brothers studio lot. Among the three of them, they must have worked on a thousand motion pictures. I don't know how many times they were nominated for Oscars. Well, Randy was their nephew. The musical genes just got shifted a little.

Randy Newman quietly went on to forge one of the most successful musical careers of recent years. Ironically, he is now in Hollywood and, like his uncles, is working in the film industry and winning Academy Award nominations. He started out as a staff songwriter for Warner Brothers, and if you want to hear some of his early work, you will find it on an old Harpers Bizarre album. The Harpers Bizarre were a very, very cute, pop-oriented singing group that had hits covering big-band standards like "Anything Goes" and "Chattanooga Choo Choo." Randy wrote a song for them called "Suzie" about a teenage girl celebrating her sixteenth birthday. The lyrics were oversweet, purposely innocuous, and anybody with a brain, not counting censors, could tell what it was about. The Harpers Bizarre may have been cute, but they sure as hell knew that underneath all the sweetness, this was a song about a girl who was going to go out and get laid for the first time. The lead singer for Harpers Bizarre eventually wound up producing Captain Beefheart records, which should tell you something.

To my mind, one of Randy Newman's first albums was one of his best, *Randy Newman: Live from the Bitter End*. Always controversial, Randy used to do a song called "Underneath a Harlem Moon." It was an old thirties song about black people from Harlem that had been recorded by Fletcher Henderson and Don Redman, among others. One of the verses to that song has a now infamous line about "why 'darkies' were born." Unfortunately for Randy, as a preview of what is now called political correctness, somebody actually beat him up outside the club for singing that ditty, and he had to take it out of his repertoire. When the controversy erupted, years later, over his song called "Short People" and all the midgets and dwarfs in the United States were up in arms, it's easy to understand why he weathered the storm so well. He already had a lot of experience.

Another interesting example of anti–political correctness was when someone in Georgia or Alabama tried to pass a law making it a crime to sing "Dixie." When Mickey Newbury heard there was such a proclamation in the works, he was playing the Bitter End West. (For a few years we tried to start a sister club out on the West Coast.) Mickey walked out onstage, told the audience about the proposed law, and then spontaneously began to sing "Dixie." He sang the first two verses and then broke into a chorus of "The Battle Hymn of the Republic," and while the audience sat in stunned silence, he ended with the final verse of "All My Sorrows." When he finished, he didn't know if he was going to be applauded or if the stage was going to be rushed. The applause was thunderous. Odetta was sitting in one of the front rows, applauding, with tears running down her cheeks. That musical montage was eventually recorded as "Amcrican Trilogy," and Mickey kept it in his act. Elvis Presley wound up recording it and having a hit with it.

While the critics were going crazy trying to put labels on all the many styles of this evolving folk-rock genre, Bitter End audiences were enjoying acts like Jerry Jeff Walker, Bill Withers, Jimmy Webb, Tom Rush, Tim Buckley, Carly Simon, David Ack-les, Gordon Lightfoot, and hundreds more. Jerry Jeff started out in a rock band called Circus Maximus, but by the time he came to the club, he was on his own and writing quiet, beautiful, introspective masterpieces like "Mr. Bojangles." Jerry was teamed up with David Bromberg, and the two of them sang and played "Mr. Bojangles" on a radio station in New York, WBAI. The disc jockey, Bob Fass, made a tape of the performance and was playing it over the air every half-hour. When Jerry came down to the club to sit in on one of the hootenannies, he played "Mr. Bojangles." It was one of the first times he played it before a live audience. People were whispering to each other excitedly, "That's the song. That's the one."

A few weeks later the *New York Times* ran a banner head-line: "Singer-Songwriters Make Comeback. Developing Trend Indicated at the Bitter End by Jerry Jeff Walker and Joni Mitchell." As word spread, the crowds began to grow and grow. One night Harry Belafonte made one of his regular stops at the club. He was intent on listening to Jerry sing "Mr. Bojangles" because Harry wanted to record it, which he eventually did. Jerry wasn't a one-hit wonder. One of my favorite Jerry Jeff songs is "My Old Man." As Jerry once told me, "That's a whole lifetime in about three and a half minutes." While Jerry beautifully sang it in the hushed silence of the Bitter End, you could see Harry Belafonte sitting in the back of the club near the soundboard, crying softly.

As it turned out, Jerry had a hell of a time getting the song recorded. Maynard Solomon of Vanguard Records didn't want to touch it. Martin Luther King had just been shot and killed. Maynard thought the song was a little bit racist. "But, Maynard," Jerry said, "it's about a white guy." Eventually it was recorded with my help and David Wilkes's, and the song has been covered successfully by everyone from Manfred Mann to Sammy Davis Jr., who turned it into a tableau for his Vegas act.

I can't imagine the summer of 1972 without Bill Withers's "Ain't No Sunshine When She's Gone." That song was coming nonstop out of radios all over the city. Bill had worked out in California for the airline industry repairing jets. His guitar playing was very rudimentary, but his poems, which he set to music, were beautifully phrased urban sonnets that captivated the nation. Bill was a terribly sweet guy with a slight stutter that vanished when he took the stage. I remember when he played the club how Bill Cosby stopped by to thank him for the songs and to tell him if he needed help with anything at all, Bill Cosby would be there for him.

The stream of talent flowed on as Jim Dawson, Jake Holmes, and Billy Joel started performing in earnest. One night Jake Holmes played a new song he wrote called "Dazed and Confused." Unbeknownst to him, the members of Led Zeppelin were in the audience and liked it so much that they went out and bought the album, altered the lyrics a little, and recorded the song. The only problem was that they never gave Jake credit or remuneration. At that time, Jake was not only performing his solo act but was also quietly becoming the most successful jingle writer in New York. He created a near-Broadway production for Coca-Cola called "I'm a Pepper, You're a Pepper" and also wrote a little tune for the U.S. Army called "Be . . . All That You Can Be." Jake wasn't hurting for money and let Led Zeppelin slide. They finally admitted the theft in their highly pretentious biography, *Hammer of the Gods*.

When Gordon Lightfoot played the club, it was something of a coup. My neighbor and nearest competitor, Howie Solomon of the Café Au Go Go, wanted Gordon Lightfoot badly. We had had a very good year to date in 1968. Neil Diamond was in and out. We had the Lemon Pipers, who had a number-one hit called "Green Tambourine," and David Steinberg was the house comic that year. I worked the phones very tenaciously and finally signed Gordon Lightfoot for a two-week gig. Howie was so mad, he ran across the street and yelled at me, "You're taking the food out of my children's mouths." The brutal irony was that during Gordon's opening week, Bobby Kennedy was killed and no one came to the shows.

By the end of the sixties, the Bitter End had a lock on comedy, folk music, folk rock, and what some people call the singer-songwriter tradition. No one could touch us. Some of the acts have been forgotten over the years, but at the time when they played the Bitter End, they were usually on top of the world. The one thing we didn't have a lock on was rock and roll. The Fillmore East was drawing big crowds. Auditoriums that normally held sporting events were booking rockers, and I felt that the Bitter End had to tap into that market. The music was good and exciting but it was very loud, and the Bitter End was too small to host Jefferson Airplane or the Doors. We had to choose slowly and wisely, and yet we needed to make a splash. For starters we tried Chuck Berry for a one-night stand. Chuck was just a little crazy and just a little too full of himself. The night of the show he showed up at the club with his guitar and that was it. "Where's my backup band?" he said. "What do you mean, where's your backup band? How the hell should I know? They're your band." Chuck wasn't fazed in the least. "I don't travel with a band. Too much money." "Well, what the hell am I supposed to do?" I asked him. "This is New York isn't it? Go find me a band," he said.

We had to run out on the street and dig up a band. Chuck's music was pretty basic rock and roll. We didn't need any virtuosos. Luckily we found Charlie Brown and Danny Armstrong hanging out, and they filled in. My many agent and manager friends were right; rock and rollers come complete with attitude. This wasn't necessarily what I had in mind. But I did finally come up with the perfect solution: the Everly Brothers.

No one could deny that the Everly Brothers were anything except rock and roll. They had about twenty top-ten records under their belt and were always mentioned in the same breath with Chuck Berry, Fats Domino, Elvis, and Jerry Lee Lewis. The Everly Brothers were in something of a bind themselves. They were having trouble making the adjustment to hard rock. After a wonderfully successful career they suddenly found themselves playing Vegas-style lounges, dressed in tuxedos, doing their classic repertoire to elderly and fading drunks. If the Bitter End needed a change, the Everly Brothers needed it more. But they didn't come cheap. I had to pay a fortune for them, and frankly I was scared to death. If this show bombed and the performances didn't sell out, or if the reviews were terrible, Fred might have been forced to fire me sooner than he did. It was a bold move, and I promoted the shows as much as I could. After paying their salaries and expenses, there was little left for anything else. From first night to last, the shows were sellouts. It was, to date, the most successful two weeks the club ever had.

Don and Phil were very professional but very stiff at first. They even dressed in their tuxes. After the second or third night Phil came over to me and said, "This is one of the most marvelous gigs we've ever done. I love it here. There's just one thing." I said, "What is that, Phil?" "Would it be all right if we didn't wear our tuxedos?" I looked at him and said, "Please."

There were good folk acts that refused to change with the times. Eric Andersen is still playing his long, deeply poetic, introspective stuff, but his audience has dwindled considerably. His song "Thirsty Boots" is still one of my favorites. I admire his tenacity and in part believe in it too, but I couldn't hold that philosophy and run a successful nightclub. Rock and roll was turning into the music of choice for most Americans. I remember in the early seventies, Eric, Dave Van Ronk, and David Buskin were having some drinks at the club and commiserating with each other over the lack of popularity of their musical enterprises. Someone mentioned "Thirsty Boots" and how that should have been a number-one record. In between resigned sighs, Van Ronk picked up a mug of beer, yanked off one of Eric Andersen's leather shoes and poured the beer into it. "Now," said Van Ronk, "Your boots won't be thirsty anymore."

7

THE SECOND-TO-THE-LAST GREAT AGE OF COMEDY

If you think there's a solution, you're part of the problem.

—**George Carlin**

THE BITTER END WAS ONE OF THE BEST springboards to fame for young comics that I ever saw. I mentioned earlier that folk music benefited from comic relief, but the opposite is also true. There is nothing worse than endless comedy. As Bitter End alumna Rita Rudner noted when a friend told her that she had been in labor for thirty-six hours, "I don't even want to do anything that feels good for thirty-six hours." Audiences become saturated and run out of laughter. It is the main drawback to comedy clubs. Two, four, six comics in a row and the audience has trouble differentiating one performer from another. By the end of the evening, they don't care anymore. Try watching five Marx Brothers movies in a row and you'll see what I mean. Laughter needs breathing space and something other than more laughter to play against to make it effective.

By the mid-sixties, the first generation of comics was moving on. Coz and Cavett became television stars, though, oddly, not as comedians at first. Coz was a dramatic star in *I Spy*, and Cavett became the intellectuals' darling of the talk-show circuit. Joan Rivers did TV and Vegas. Woody Allen and Richie Pryor settled into television and eventually the movies. At the end of the summer of 1964, Richie did a gig at the Bitter End. He was a smash, especially when he pretended to be a fertilized human egg on its journey through nine months of fetal development. I think Miles Davis was there that night. That's not important. What was important was that a talent scout for the *Rudy Vallee Show* was in the audience, and a week later Richie was on the map.

There was a lot more freedom of expression for comics by the mid-sixties. Lenny Bruce had been arrested for obscenity in 1964 at the Café Au Go Go, right across the street from the Bitter End. My good friend and favorite competitor, Howie Solomon, the owner of the Au Go Go, was arrested with him, so that bust affected all of us club owners. The ordeal would cost Lenny a fortune in legal bills and cruelly drive him deeper and deeper into the despair and drug addiction that would eventually kill him. It was a cowardly persecution by the police and the federal government. Other comics were using obscenity and becoming more daring, but little or nothing happened to them. All the sights were telescopically pointing at Lenny. In an odd way, he was the Pete Seeger of comedy. From the vantage point of Bleecker Street you could see the unfairness of it all. Many of Lenny's protégés were performing with impunity, and you had the feeling that the government knew it was going to lose the war it was waging in the name of public decency, but if they were going down, they were going to take Lenny with them. In the end, of course, they failed. Lenny not only became a major influence on a lot of young comedians but he became a martyr as well.

Two of Lenny's protégés were a couple of British kids that used to listen to him on bootlegged record versions back in England. Their names were Nick Ullett and Tony Hendra. While Jackie Mason was performing in England, he heard them and promised to help them if they ever came to the States. "Who knows," said Jackie, "you guys might become the Beatles of comedy." They took him up on his offer, and on their first evening in America in the fall of 1964, Hendra and Ullett made their U.S. debut at the Bitter End, where they were a sensation. After that great beginning, the boys never did establish themselves as comic geniuses, although better things would follow. They did manage a few spots on the *Ed Sullivan Show,* and they got to see their hero, Lenny Bruce, in person a couple of times at the Au Go Go before the cops moved in. Tony Hendra would go on to create the *National Lampoon* and actually bring a comedy group from the magazine back to the club about ten years later. He has gained a kind of immortality by writing and starring (Tony was the manager) in the faux documentary *Spinal Tap,* while Nick Ullett would have great success in musical comedy on Broadway.

But not every comic was influenced by Lenny, as some biographers like to claim. Dick Cavett didn't see the point of it at all. David Brenner was more influenced by his vaudevillian father, Lou, than anyone else; and Robert Klein's humor was more affected by Jonathan Winters's rather than Lenny's approach. Most comics who tried to imitate Lenny usually failed. Worse still, after Lenny was busted, there were actually some comics who stole his material line for line. These guys were scorned by most of the Village, and a couple of times Lenny's friends would boo them off the stage and threaten to slug them. While all this was going on, there was a pleasant increase in female comics. It was still a rarity but it was a growing concern. One of the most interesting was Tracy Newman.

Tracy came east from California with her then boyfriend, folksinger Barry McGuire, who had a hit record called "Eve of Destruction." Tracy played guitar and used to dress up like a British horse-riding instructor with jodhpurs and a hat like the bobbies would wear. She was one of the first people to ever cover the Beatles professionally, and fans like Bob Dylan and Phil Ochs used to come to the club to hear her perform. When she first started out, her act consisted of ten minutes of talk and forty minutes of music. After a year of performing, her act had become ten minutes of music and forty minutes of talk. Eventually she discarded the guitar and just did stand-up. She immersed herself in the New York comedy scene doing gigs at the Bitter End and then hanging out, late into the night, uptown with the boys at the Improv.

Tracy eventually returned to California, where she was one of the founding members of the Groundlings, an improvisational comedy school. When Lorne Michaels came West to cast his new television show *Saturday Night Live,* he auditioned members of the Groundlings. Tracy was more interested in writing and teaching than performing, but her little sister, Laraine Newman, was hired as part of the original cast. Tracy would go on to work in television and would eventually win an Emmy for writing the "coming out" episode of *Ellen.*

Tracy was really unique. In the beginning there just weren't that many female stand-ups. The ones who were working, like Phyllis Diller, Joanne Worley, Ruth Buzzi, and Kaye Ballard, were based in the uptown theater clubs and thought of themselves as comic actresses or comic singers. They were very good at what they did, but they had little appeal for the younger crowd. A very special exception to that group was a comic named Maury Hayden. In fact, during the writing of this book, Tracy Newman asked us to mention Maury and how much of an influence she was on all the young girls just starting out. Her real name was Marlene, and she came from a wealthy Philadelphia family. She gave that all up to try her luck in the Village. Maury had a hard life, but her influence was real and continuous, not only with girls like Tracy and Lily Tomlin but right up to comics like Sandra Bernhardt. She evolved into a playwright, author, performance artist, singer, and pianist as well as an influential comic. She later changed her name to Lotus Weinstock. "Angels can fly because they take themselves lightly" was one of my favorite lines.

When the folk music parodists Allen and Grier, who were really Jake and Kay Holmes, broke up because of infidelity, their agent and partial cause of the breakup, Roy Silver, tried to keep the act going. He paired Kay with another male singer who could do comedy, Weston Gavin, but apparently Kay found the whole experience too ghastly and resigned. Roy wouldn't quit and decided to keep Weston and replace Kay with Maury Hayden. It was one of Maury's first breaks. Someone once described her as a woman who knew how God worked but not her ATM card. She was engaged to Lenny Bruce at the time of his death. After that tragedy, she joined a cult because, as she said, "It was the only therapy I could afford." She was famous for a routine called "The Ten-Step Program" on how to attract a man. "One of my goals is to be the most noncompetitive woman in the world!"

She was diagnosed with a brain tumor about five years ago, which caused her to reembrace Judaism to the point where she even threatened to get a reverse nose job and put the bump back on. "When I see a space, I have to fill it," she once said. Her personalized bumper sticker read "I Brake for Insights." Lotus died August 31, 1997. The tribute at the Improv to celebrate her life had David Zasloff playing "My Funny Valentine" on the shofar. Sandra Bernhardt, Budd Friedman, Phil Proctor, Julia Sweeney, and many more contemporary writers and comics attended. There are still a few copies of her book, *The Lotus Position,* in circulation. Her daughter, Lily, is one of the finest concert violinists working in America.

Another great woman comic to play the club was Lily Tomlin. She originally worked with Richmond Shepard in his mime troupe back in the early sixties. This was an enormous aid in the subtle physical comedy that she wound up doing later on at the club, like Suzy Sorority and the telephone operator who kept driving Gore Vidal crazy. Lily always had crazy ideas, special performances for kids, free shows, and giveaways. It usually almost never worked but we did the best we could. Television producers and talent scouts had permanent seats back in those days, and Lily was quickly picked up by the *Laugh-In* people, where she became a regular. She later used that experience to establish herself on Broadway, but it wasn't easy. Lily reminisced, "There was not much comedy in the 1970s, so few women. When I first went to the Bitter End, I was considered very hip and advanced. Then after I had done *Laugh-In,* I returned to New York to do theater again, and people said 'What're you gonna do? You're a TV star!' There was this tremendous reverse snobbery." It was just never easy for women comics.

Still another young comic who was picked up by Hollywood was Bud Cort. The interesting thing about Bud was that he had to be rediscovered. He got a very early start in the movies as an extra in *Up the Down Staircase* in 1967. Nothing happened after that, so he went back to acting school and got work in the soaps. I don't know whether it was because he was dating Elaine May's daughter or because he was hanging out with Timothy

Leary, but he finally put together a stand-up comedy routine and played the Bitter End. Lily Tomlin used to drive him home late at night because he was only a kid at the time. But while he was working in the Village, Robert Altman saw him and immediately cast him in *M*A*S*H* and later on in *Brewster McCloud* and *Harold and Maude*.

Comedy is a very tough business, especially at the Bitter End level. There is no place to hide on our stage. Few people have the temerity to stick it out. And if they do make it, or if offers for movies and television come in, they leave and seldom return. There are others, however, who are born to work a room. David Brenner is a good example. Another one is Robert Klein. Bobby Klein was all New York. He came out of the Bronx and, like Dick Cavett, went to Yale to study acting. This was an enormous bonus for Robert because a lot of his comedy had a stream-of-consciousness style and depended on the seemingly spontaneous emergence of weird characters that would pop out of his mouth in the middle of a bit. One of my favorite characters is the old black musician who can't stop his leg from moving while he plays the blues on his harmonica. When Robert first came to the club in the mid-sixties, he was the opening act for two old black bluesmen named Sonny Terry and Brownie McGhee. Sonny and Brownie were a team since 1939 and played all over the world until Sonny's death in 1986. Brownie played guitar, and Sonny, who was blind, played harmonica. By the time I knew them, they hated each other and wouldn't even speak to each other backstage. Bobby Klein loved them, and if he didn't learn blues harp from Sonny, then he sure as hell picked up a lot of good licks. Brownie and Sonny used to call each other River. One night Robert asked Brownie why he called Sonny River. Brownie said, "'Cause he just keeps goin' on and on and on."

In 1966, for some reason that I forget now, we decided to

book a mentalist named Dr. Richard Ireland, and Robert Klein was the opening act. Dr. Ireland was one of those guys who would blindfold himself and then tell you what was in your wallet and where to find your missing car keys. Of course he made it all seem supernatural, and Robert, like Johnny Carson, never admired that kind of act because these guys, for publicity, would always up the ante. Sure enough, right before he opened for us, Dr. Ireland went on the radio and claimed he could also cure people, that he was some kind of healer. It was a bunch of bullshit, but it was an unexpected bonanza for the club. Opening night we had lines around the block, with people who were lame and on crutches and in wheelchairs. It was like Lourdes. And here's poor Bobby Klein trying to do his jokes for ill people. I thought Ireland was harmless enough, and he had a good sense of humor. People would catch him going up to the Tin Angel for a bite to eat and say, "What am I thinking about?" and Ireland would say, "I knew you were going to ask me that." During his run, Jake Holmes and Tim Rose had their guitars stolen and figured, "What the hell." They went to one of the shows and sent a message to Ireland in a folded piece of paper. Ireland held the paper up to his forehead and said, "Ah, the guitars are in the hall closet," or something equally stupid. When Jake and Tim went to wherever Ireland told them to go, of course the guitars weren't there. When they told him about their failure, he said, "Ah, someone must have got there first." As Robert Klein and anybody with a brain understood, it was all about clever ways of peeking through the blindfold. But desperate people will do anything, and that was what Robert couldn't stand.

Somehow Robert's Bitter End gigs were always tougher than they should have been. In 1972 I booked, well in advance, an up-and-coming band named America. By the time their date arrived they had the number-one record in America, "A Horse with No

Name." They were the opening act for a three-act show with Robert Klein as the headliner, and again there were lines around the block. But because America was the opening act, they were only due to be on for about thirty minutes. The only trouble was that 90 percent of the audience had come to hear the band with the number-one song. They weren't interested in any of the other performers, so when Robert came on, the house would always be half full.

Robert studied at Second City, where Alan Arkin and John Brent cut their acting and comedic teeth. This led to numerous roles on Broadway. Bobby's most memorable roles included playing opposite Lucie Arnaz in *They're Playing Our Song,* for which he received a Tony nomination, and *The Sisters Rosenweig,* for which he won the Obie and Outer Critics Circle Award for Outstanding Performance by an Actor. Besides his Bitter End performances, my favorite Robert Klein bit occurred when he hosted *Saturday Night Live* and starred in the first of the famous "Cheeseburger" sketches with John Belushi and Dan Aykroyd. "It was great for a young comic like me to play the Bitter End because after the show I'd walk outside and Paul or Fred would be talking to Jack Rollins or Charlie Joffe. They would offer advice, and I took a lot of it. But the main thing was that these guys were players. They were really in the business, and that was all very exciting and important to someone still trying to make it."

A lot of very creative people used comedy as a shoehorn to help them slide into show business. Comics like Howie Storm started performing at hoots all over the Village. I heard Howie and many other entertainers describe their steady gigs at the Village clubs as similar to going to the gymnasium: a place where you could work things out onstage. Howie, or Howard, Storm, as he likes to be called now, worked at the Bitter End into the mid-sixties and then began discovering himself first as an actor and then as a writer and director. Woody hired him for a role in *Take the Money and Run* in 1969. It wasn't long before he began writing and directing for television.

Another actor-comic who showed up at the club every once in a while was John Brent. John was a friend of Lotus Weinstock's and was one of the most insane men you'd ever want to meet. Like his friend Wavy Gravy, John started out as a poet and got into acting and comedy later on when he joined Second City. He used the Bitter End as a platform for whatever was on his mind and never really had an act that managers could use and develop. John's "act" was being John. He was a moocher without peer and would constantly house-sit for, and then hose, his friends. When the friends returned, they would often find most of their belongings missing, with pawn-ticket stubs stuck in the freezer or stuffed under a mattress. John would usually be resting comfortably on the sofa in his host's underwear, complaining that he was out of food. Howard Hesseman of *WKRP* fame once told this story: When Wavy Gravy was playing the shaman at the Woodstock festival, he found a broken dorgi, which was some kind of Eastern religious charm, and took it to Hesseman's wife, who made jewelry out of dental wax. Wavy asked her if she could weld the thing together. John Brent was with him, and the two of them watched as she worked on it. There was a terrible storm raging outside with lots of thunder and lightning. Just as she was finishing the welding job, a violent thunderclap exploded, and the two halves of the dorgi seemed to magically, or at least magnetically, jump at each other. Wavy was convinced he had witnessed a genuine religious experience. John leaped up and screamed "Yes! This experience makes me feel like Thor!" and he grabbed a hammer and smashed the dorgi in two again while Wavy wept. There is little left of John Brent, who died at a very young age, very little written and nothing that I know of on video, but somewhere there are a few copies of a privately printed book of his poems called *All Grief Be Far*. If you ever find a copy, treasure it.

During the summer months, when business was sometimes slow, there was always a lot of leeway given to comics. Agents would use the time to develop routines and bits, and the comics got a lot of experience. Our comic in residence back in 1967 was David Steinberg. David was a Canadian and supposedly the son of a rabbi. That's not the only thing he was a son of, but I guess you can't like everybody. When David left home for anywhere but a life in the synagogue, his father apparently said, "I kiss the train that takes you away." David was one of those guys who were smitten with Lenny Bruce, but, to his credit, he created some very original material. He tried to work with Second City, but David was not a good improvisational comic and his stay with the troupe didn't last long. The Bitter End was the perfect spot for David because David was a much better writer than he was a performer. There was a superciliousness about his delivery that annoyed a lot of people. He could be very irreverent, especially when he talked about religion. One of the bits he used to do at the club about a holier-than-thou minister was performed on the *Smothers Brothers Comedy Hour*. That was David's big break. The performance so outraged people that the show and the sponsors were deluged with hate mail. Tom and Dick loved it and made David a semiregular until the show was finally thrown off the air. The success went to David's head, and he got to be hard to be around. He was the kind of guy who never looked back.

When David first came to the club, Fred either couldn't stand him or just got tired of him. Fred was very fickle about comics. During the summer of 1968, Fred went on an African safari with Ted Ashley. These two would eventually be responsible for bringing Woodstock to the screen. Fred was gone for over a month, and when he got back, one of the first things he said to me was, "What the fuck is Steinberg still here for? Get rid of him." I told Fred that David was going to be very big. A lot of industry people liked him. I had a big argument with Fred, but I stuck to my guns. I stood up for David Steinberg, and, sure enough, eventually the success happened that I knew would be his. Later, when he was playing in Los Angeles, I stopped by with some friends to see him. He pretended he didn't know me. Made me buy my own tickets and was very cold when I stopped by his dressing room. He didn't need Paul Colby and the Bitter End anymore. I thought it was a lousy thing to do to someone who helped make his reputation. I thought it was a lousy thing to do to someone who stood up for him.

David skyrocketed for a couple of years, and everybody held out great hopes for him. He was even talked about as a replacement for Johnny Carson and guest hosted the show once or twice, but he was always a little too full of himself. He eventually dropped out of the public eye. He is now one of the most respected and award-winning writers and directors in television today. He won a couple of Emmys for writing Billy Crystal's lines during the Oscars, and he's received even more awards for his directing work on shows like *Friends, Mad about You,* and *Seinfeld.*

He used to do a bit about a psychiatrist who would tell clients to sit down on any number of different chairs. Wherever the client sat down, the shrink would yell, "Ah ha! Oedipus complex," or "I see, paranoid schizophrenia." The psychiatrist would keep saying, "Remember, everything counts." I can't help thinking of that line when I think of David.

Fred Weintraub, who was spending a lot of time out of the

club, was still insistent about placing his own acts or performers that he took a shine to personally. This was never really a problem, because Fred had good taste. Most of the time. I think it was around 1967 that he brought in the Fabulous Pickle Brothers. The only problem was that they were not fabulous. I think Fred liked them because they were a comedy group. Fred loved sketch comics, and the more the merrier. It was why he was so keen on Jim, Jake and Joan. The Pickle Brothers soon metamorphosed into the Uncalled Four, which eventually became the Uncalled-for Three. Before long we had one troupe after another performing at the club. My favorite was the Ace Trucking Company.

The Aces had a great time at the club, and most of them doubled as part-time help. George Terry and Mike Mislove often emceed the hoots or the special comedy nights we were sponsoring. I forget what Fred Willard did, but Billy Saluga was our doorman for a while. Bill Saluga had a character that he called Raymond J. Johnson Jr. Bill would dress up in a zoot suit and a porkpie hat. He would usually have someone interview him and ask him his name. That was all it took. "My name is Raymond J. Johnson Jr. But youse don't have to call me Johnson. Youse can call me Ray or youse can call me Jay or youse can call me Ray Jay or youse can call me Jay Ray," ad nauseam, ad infinitum. I don't know why, I don't know how, but that was one of the funniest routines I ever heard. Bill went on television and did the same act. People couldn't get enough of him. By the seventies, when the disco craze was going strong, Bill cut an album called *Dancing Johnson*. While a disco beat played endlessly and some chicks sang a goofy chorus in the background, Bill would talk over them, "Now youse don't have to call me Johnson. Youse can call me Ray . . ." I saw people at parties, at the slightest provocation, start doing Bill's bit, and the amazing thing was that it always got a laugh. David Steinberg took him out to Hollywood and got him a lot exposure. Recently he's been on TV shows like *Mad about You* and *Seinfeld*.

When David Brenner came to the club in the late sixties, he was of two minds whether or not to pursue a career in show business. College offered other options in the communications field, and David had already written and produced over a hundred documentary films for Westinghouse and Metromedia Broadcasting. David came from a tough Philadelphia neighborhood and was headed for a highly successful career behind the camera. His greatest influence, his dad, Lou Brenner, was a premier vaudevillian who Milton Berle said was the funniest man he ever knew. David simply had to give showbiz a shot.

When he started out in New York, there were few places for beginners to perform comedy, so it was only natural that he start at the Bitter End. David was very funny and sometimes off-color, but his routines were very intelligent and loaded with references for New York hipsters. Then two events changed David's career. The first event occurred at the Bitter End. A talent scout for the *Tonight Show* stopped in to hear David's act. David was killing the audience, but his material was very hip and risqué. After the show, David's agent introduced him to the talent scout, and the scout remarked about David's "toilet" material. It was a disaster. David was understandably miffed. "Why didn't you tell me he was in the audience?" said David. "I would have tailored my material." The other event happened a little later.

David used to rip the government apart, which was standard operating procedure back in the sixties, until one night outside of the Improv he met Rodney Dangerfield. Rodney said, "Hey, I saw you tonight, and you're pretty good kid, pretty good. Let me ask you a question. What percent of America do you think is hip?" "Well, at the most I guess 10 percent," said David. "Yeah, you got a very hip act," Rodney continued. "You know what? You can take the 10 percent, and I'll take the 90 percent."

After the "toilet" material incident and talking to Rodney that night, David took all the hip stuff right out of his act. He asked himself if he was in this racket to make money or to impress someone. "I realized," said David, "one night when I was doing my hip stuff, that when I made fun of the liberals, the whole audience screamed. When I made fun of the conservatives, only the liberals would laugh."

Anyway, the talent scout came back, and David did a hysterical but clean act, thoroughly unhip, and on January 8, 1971, he made the first of 158 appearances on the *Tonight Show*. He would eventually host the show a record 75 times. David went on to appear on more talk shows than any other entertainer in America, and it all started at the Bitter End.

David stayed close to the Village and kept working on his material. As Bill Cosby once remarked, television eats up material faster than any other medium. Before David would do a *Tonight Show,* I would always put him onstage for a week and let him practice his bits or his monologue. David was tireless, especially just before a TV appearance. He would do two shows at the Bitter End, and in between shows he would run around the Village trying to get on any stage that would have him for a couple of minutes. One night he finished his set at the club and ran around the corner to the Champagne Gallery next to the Sullivan Street Playhouse. He went up to the emcee and said, "Hi, I'm David Brenner, the comedian?" Nothing. "I'm working at the Bitter End, and I'm getting ready for the *Tonight Show.*" Again no response. "I just want to practice my monologue. If I could get eight minutes I'd appreciate it." The emcee said, "You work at the Bitter End?" "Yeah, I'm right around the corner. I'm on the marquee—David Brenner." "Well, I never saw you before," said the emcee. "I've done three *Tonight Show's,*" said David. "Just give me eight minutes. I've got to practice this monologue because I'm on next Tuesday."

So the emcee shrugs and gets up onstage. There was a folksinger due up, but the emcee grabbed the mike and said, "We have a young man now who says he's working at the Bitter End. I don't know if he's working at the Bitter End. I didn't walk by the Bitter End, you know, I didn't see his name out there or anything. Maybe he is working at the Bitter End, I don't know. He says he's doing the *Tonight Show* next Tuesday. Says he's done it before. I never saw him on the *Tonight Show*. I don't know if he's ever done the *Tonight Show*. He's a comedian. At least he says he's a comedian. I don't know, I never saw him before. He says his name is David Brenner." He kept going on and on. Finally, he said, "Here he is, David Brenner." So David walked out on the stage and instead of practicing his monologue, he said, "I want to thank the emcee for that introduction. I don't know if he is an emcee. I never saw him emcee before. He says he's an emcee. He came up here onstage. He started talking into the mike. Usually only emcees can talk into the mike. I never saw him talk into a mike before." On and on for eight minutes, and then David went back to the Bitter End and did his next set.

"There was never a night, even if it was only a hootenanny night, that you didn't see hordes of industry people in the audience," said David. "The Bitter End was *the* room in New York City for comedy."

David ran into some personal problems over custody of his child. He practically stopped working for a couple of years and eventually won the case in court. He's always on the circuit and grins wryly when he hears his material coming out of the mouths of other comics. "My material must be contemporary, because people keep stealing it." As he said recently, "There are some superstar comedians who haven't had an original word

Paul Colby and Linda Ronstadt on the Bitter End stage circa 1968, during her appearance with the Stone Poneys. *Photographer unknown.*

Neil Diamond with Jeremy Steig and Paul Colby in the late sixties. Neil Diamond was managed by Fredanna, the management
company started by original Bitter End owner Fred Weintraub.
Photographer unknown.

Paul Colby with Arlo Guthrie and sixties folk heartthrob Melanie during Arlo's performance, which was later released as a live recording. *Courtesy of Peter Cunningham.*

Paul Colby, John Denver, and Tom Paxton circa 1971, when Denver reinvented himself as a solo artist after Peter, Paul and Mary recorded his song "Leavin' on a Jet Plane" and took it to number one. *Courtesy of RCA.*

Bob Dylan, Paul Colby, and Ramblin' Jack Elliott during rehearsals at the Bitter End for the Rolling Thunder Revue, circa 1975. *Courtesy of Ruth Bernel.*

Paul Colby and Carly Simon on her triumphant return to the Bitter End as star soloist in the early seventies. Carly and sister Lucy first played the club a decade earlier as the Simon Sisters, opening for Bill Cosby and Woody Allen. © *Bob Gruen*.

Andy Gibb and Paul Colby, while Gibb was appearing at the Bitter End the week his record "I Just Want to Be Your Everything" went number one. Andy's agent tried to cancel the gig, but Andy said, "No way. Paul Colby believed in me before anybody." *Courtesy Lynn Goldsmith.*

Paul Colby, Bill Withers, and friend. Bill Withers conquered the music world in 1972 with "Ain't No Sunshine." Bill Cosby often stopped by the club to listen and lend support. © *Bob Gruen.*

Allen Ginsberg, Paul Colby, and fan during the week of Ginsberg's performance in the late seventies. Ginsberg sang and chanted his poetry to the accompaniment of a small band and the strumming of his own esoteric musical instruments. *Courtesy of Ebet Roberts.*

Paul Colby, Marshall Chapman, and Andy Warhol when Warhol stopped by the club to hear Chapman, who was known as the female Mick Jagger. In response to Warhol's famous dictum on fifteen minutes of fame, Colby asked him for a whole hour. *Photographer unknown.*

Paul Colby and Judy Collins, June 1997, recalling old times at a music awards show. *Courtesy of Chuck Pulin.*

Tommy James at the Bitter End in the late 1990s during the live recording of his greatest hits. The event, captured on CD and filmed for video, eventually became one of the first-ever DVD releases. *Courtesy Chuck Pulin.*

Paul Colby and Pete Seeger at the first fund-raising concert for the Folk Music Museum in Greenwich Village in summer 2000. *Courtesy of Tom Senif.*

The front door of the Bitter End opening onto Bleecker Street as it looks today and as it has essentially looked since its 1961 opening.

ONE NIGHT ONLY, THE LEGENDARY
CHUCK BERRY
WED., SEPT. 27
9:00 & 10:30 SHOWS · Reservations required
BITTER END
147 Bleecker St. · GR 5-7804

APPEARING NOW FOR ONE WEEK ONLY—
JAMES TAYLOR
Apple Recording Artist
COMING NEXT WEEK: **TOM PAXTON**
(For one week only)
COMING MAY 30th: The EVERLY BROS.
FRED WEINTRAUB & PAUL COLBY
BITTER END · 147 BLEECKER STREET
GREENWICH VILLAGE, N.Y. · RES. GR 5-7804

NOW THROUGH APRIL 3
STEVIE WONDER
TAMLA MOTOWN RECORDING ARTIST
Plus **BOBBY WHITLOCK**
DUNHILL RECORDING ARTIST
Coming **CEECH & CHONG** Plus . . .
HARRY CHAPIN EASTER WEEK APRIL 5 to 10
MIMI FARINA & TOM JANS April 12 to 17
Bette Midler MAY 10 THROUGH 15 BY ADVANCE TICKET SALE ONLY AT BITTER END OFFICE
FRED WEINTRAUB & PAUL COLBY
Talent Showcase Every Tuesday
BITTER END · 147 BLEECKER STREET / GR 5-7804
GREENWICH VILLAGE N.Y.

come out of their mouths their whole career, but I don't care. I can create faster than they can steal." David told me that he's like a jazz saxophonist. He sets his index cards on a table or piano top with thoughts and sketch ideas written down, and then he just leans back and wails. "I guess one of my contributions is the file cards with ideas written down to play off of. A lot of comics work that way, and so do I. Except now the lettering is a lot bigger."

Jimmie Walker started out at the hoots, and he used to drive me crazy. He had a day job writing copy for a radio station, and he was getting laughs. He tried to parlay that into a stand-up career and started doing open-mike nights. He was pretty bad, but we always gave comics endless chances because there were so few of them. By 1969 David Brenner was securing his reputation and was able to help a lot of the new comics who followed him into the Bitter End. David took Jimmie and Steve Landesberg and made sure they got regular gigs at the Improv, where they became regulars. When he gained a foothold on the *Tonight Show,* he did the same thing. Once on the Jack Paar show, David, Steve Landesberg, and Bette Midler, all scheduled guests, refused to go on unless Jimmie Walker got a guest shot. The Paar staff unbelievably caved in. He then went on to appear in a new comedy series *Good Times,* where *Time* magazine named him Comedian of the Decade. Jimmie's hard work made him become very good.

I must say that among performers, I found comics to be the most generous and least selfish people. Everyone in that world always seems to pull for each other. Bill Cosby came back to the Bitter End in the early seventies, not to perform, but to hold impromptu comedy workshops. I remember he took a little passport photo of himself, pasted it on a piece of paper, and announced a press conference at the club. He mimeographed a couple of dozen copies and handed them out. This was the beginning of his workshop. One of those attending was Steve Landesberg. Steve was a good friend of David Brenner's, and David knew he was hysterical, but he had yet to do an open-mike night anywhere. After listening to Coz, he found the courage and went on to perform and become another Bitter End alumni success story.

Not everyone started at the Bitter End. Some comics would come East from California or elsewhere. Usually they had yet to make a name for themselves, and so the Bitter End was a necessary stop. Albert Brooks was one of those. Like David Brenner, he had a father who was in show business. Albert's father, Harry Einstein, was a radio–big-band comic who went under the name Parkyakarkus. In the age when ethnic humor was king, Harry was the only guy who played a Greek. I always thought Albert was crazy to change his name from Einstein to Brooks. Just once I wanted to say, "Ladies and gentlemen, the Bitter End is proud to introduce . . . Albert Einstein!" Albert did two weeks for us, and he was very strange.

Albert's humor was unique, to say the least. He would get up onstage with a couple of those bowling pins that jugglers use and say, "Ladies and gentlemen, I perfected this juggling act with my brother last year, and it takes a lot of concentration." He would then start turning the pins over in his hand. "Very difficult. Needs lots of control. So here we go." And then he would throw the pins underhanded against the red brick wall, where they would crash to the ground. "Of course," he would then say, "it works a lot better when my brother is here." He perfected that kind of comedy. I remember him working on a bit that he couldn't do at the club but that wound up on one of his Ed Sullivan appearances. Ed Sullivan always had a plate spinner. This was a guy who would have about fifty plates, and fifty long rods coming up out of the floor. He would then take the plates and one by one get them spinning. Of course in the midst of the act, the spinning plates would begin to wobble and slow down and threaten to fall to the ground. So the guy was constantly running back and forth keeping everything going until he had all fifty spinning at once. Well, Albert did the same act except he used volunteers and jokes instead of plates and sticks. He would line up a dozen people and one by one start telling them stupid jokes. They would laugh uproariously, and Albert would go on with the next person and the next joke. But before he could get to the end, the jokes would start to wear off on the first bunch of people, and so he'd have to run back and tell them more jokes and get them laughing again. He even had the orchestra play Khachaturian's *Dance of the Sabres* until, finally, he had all the volunteers laughing at once. It was one of the dumbest and funniest things I ever saw.

Albert actually came just before David Brenner hit it big. On one of the nights that Albert was performing, David and Steve Landesberg were in the audience. They watched the show, loved it, and thought Albert was a genius. And they followed him back to the dressing room after the show. Albert listened to them for a second and said, "Could you guys wait a minute while I go to the bathroom?" The boys said sure. David and Steve then stood outside the men's room for about a half-hour until it suddenly dawned on them that Albert wasn't ever coming out. At least not while they were there.

I had my own weird run-in with Albert. Albert was very concerned with money. His manager stood by the door with a clicker to count the number of people coming to see the show. Albert wasn't going to get cheated. This drove me crazy because it was an insult to me. I don't know where Albert had played before, but the Bitter End and I had a reputation for being up-front with artists. Anyway, after the end of the engagement, Albert came up to the office for his money. I gave it to him and told him how I had arrived at the figure. It was not the route that Albert and his manager took, and they assumed that I was cheating them. We sat for an hour. Albert kept insisting X amount of people came in and he was due X amount of money based on X amount of people, etc. I realized that we were coming at the head count from two different directions but in the end it was the same amount of money. I finally got so annoyed that I said, "Okay, Albert, have it your way. If your arithmetic says I owe you this amount of money, then that's what I'm going to pay you." They were flabbergasted. "That's really nice of you," said Albert with a wink at his agent. "I really admire that." My secretary came over to me and said, "What are you doing?" I whispered, "Don't worry." After Albert left, I showed her the numbers. "They're exactly the same," she said. "I know," I said. I never bothered telling Albert, and to this day I guess he thinks he really got one over on me.

Albert went on to write and perform for the Smothers Brothers' show where so many of the Bitter End regulars wound up. He is now one of those rare, self-contained Hollywood engines that write, produce, direct, and often star in their own feature-length films. Whoever said comedians had to be normal?

This seems as good a place as any to remention Bill Cosby. Bill always stayed close to the Bitter End. I mentioned that he would stop by quite often to watch favorite acts like Curtis Mayfield and Bill Withers. He also ran comedy workshops to help young stand-ups get started. But there was also an unpleasant connection to the Bitter End that surfaced in the late sixties, and I want to set things straight for the record. When Bill first started out, he played other clubs besides the Bitter End. One of his favorite spots was the Gaslight. The Gaslight has a lot of wonderful history connected to it and actually predates the Bitter End by a couple of years. Bill not only played the Gaslight but also his apartment was in the same building. John Mitchell was the original owner; he eventually sold it to Clarence and Sam Hood.

One night early in his career, Bill invited Clarence and Sam to the Bitter End to see his act. This was very common. Club owners were always showing up at each other's place. Well, on one particular night in 1962, the Hoods made a tape of Bill's performance. Bill let them do it with the understanding that it was to be a private memento. Well, by the late sixties, Bill Cosby was as hot as a star could be. He was an Emmy-winning TV star and the first black actor to costar with a white male lead. He had produced a dozen comedy albums, and all of them sold in the millions. At the same time, the Hoods fell on hard luck. Somebody remembered the tape made at the Bitter End and decided they were sitting on a fortune. The Hoods, a lawyer, and Bill Cosby's first manager, Sam Guard, started hawking the tape to rival record labels. Bill got wind of the scheme and sued. Bill reiterated that the tape was meant as a private memento and that it was a very early example of his work. There were sloppy and amateurish moments on the tape, and he didn't want the whole world to hear it now. The case eventually went to the state supreme court, and Bill won. As the story appeared in the newspapers, the tapes were always referred to as the Bitter End tapes. The Bitter End, however, had nothing to do with it. No one connected with the club ever taped anyone without their knowledge. Maybe that's why Bill stayed in touch with the club all those years.

For a while the Bitter End was the home to the most zany comedy duos. Comedy teams are the hardest acts to keep together. The work is hard, the tensions never cease, and the marriages are often rocky. I mentioned Hendra and Ullett, Allen and Grier, and Jim, Jake and Joan, but there were plenty of others. The Times Square Two were one of my favorites. These guys were Englishmen and dressed like music-hall vaudevillians. They wore twenties-style dark suits, greased and parted their hair down the middle, and affected glasses. They were British nerds. They played comic songs with a very dry sense of humor. But if the song didn't work, they backed it up with hysterical presentations. They would pass a single guitar back and forth between them, playing behind their backs, under their legs, moving it so that one was making the chords while the other did the strumming and picking. They would litter the stage with props and wacky instruments. They had two little dolls made up to look like them and would play with them on stage. They were so eccentric that the Mothers of Invention invited them on one of their tours as opening act.

Tom Pachett and Jay Tarses were another comedy team. I think Tarses was a truck driver until he hooked up with Pachett and started writing jokes. They were very satirical and brooding, but for the life of me I can't remember a single bit they did. I asked some other comics if they remembered them, and I got the same response. David Brenner said they were like bagels and cream cheese. Not filet mignon but filling. They worked out their bits at the Bitter End and became comic scientists. They could tell you how to be funny, they could write funny things, but they couldn't quite succeed on their own as performers. So they did the next best thing. They moved to Hollywood and became Emmy-Award-winning writers and producers. They wrote for the *Carol Burnett Show*, the *Bob Newhart Show*. They created *ALF* and *Buffalo Bill*, ran MTM TV's production company, and created work as different as *The Muppet Movie* and *The Days and Nights of Molly Dodd*. Jay's daughter until a few years ago was an executive for ABC Entertainment. In Hollywood, even with all their success, they are still branded as "dark comedy" writers.

Another group from England was the Scaffold. The Scaffold was a sketch-comedy group that included Mike McCartney, who went by the name of Mike McGear because he never wanted to appear to capitalize on his brother Paul's name. It would have been a lot easier to promote the act if we could have gotten out the fact that Mike was the brother of one of the Beatles. But that was a family issue, and you have to respect that. The Scaffold worked with Peter Cook and Dudley Moore. They teamed up with Neil Innes from the Bonzo Dog Band and did a lot of work for British TV. They were very shy and a little scared when they played. I remember they picked up a hitchhiker one night after leaving the club, and it turned out to be Buzzy Linhart, who knew the Beatles. Buzzy became their tour guide and showed them all over the city. The Scaffold were a real throwback to the old days at the club and weren't afraid to lace their act with poetry and music. Mike wrote very popular Christmas songs in the late sixties, but they only succeeded in England. Even so, there is a recording somewhere of Jack Bruce, Graham Nash, and Reggie Dwight doing a holiday song called "Lily the Pink" with Mike pounding on Ringo Starr's bass drum to keep up the beat. Reggie Dwight, by the way, later changed his name to Elton John.

By the end of the sixties the Bitter End was the hippest place to see and hear comedy. Sometimes I could kill two birds with one stone with acts like Arlo Guthrie, who was as funny a comic as he was talented as a singer and composer. Not quite so talented but very amusing was Biff Rose. He played piano and made a slew of albums that a lot of people bought very quickly and then promptly forgot why. He became oversaturated, although he did well when he played for me. That might have been because I had him open for Jackson Browne. Biff was an unabashed hippie. My favorite song of his was "You Can Take the Country Out of Marijuana But You Can't Take Marijuana Out of the Country." Biff is still out there playing the piano, making up crazy, extemporaneous songs à la Steve Allen. He has a girlfriend who does quick sketches, and together they travel the hotels and resorts like the uncle and the niece in *Night of the Iguana,* and I hear they make a nice living. The live album he made at the club is still out there in vinyl-record shops.

Our best act by the end of the sixties was my good friend George Carlin. George's story was unique. George, more than any of the other great comics, really had to transform himself from one kind of entertainer to another. I can't think of anyone else who changed so dramatically. I remember one day in the mid-sixties I started getting calls from an agent named Jeff Wald. Jeff represented George Carlin at the time. Now I knew about George. I had seen George on television and in a few supper clubs. He was what I would characterize as an uptown act. He wasn't a Bitter End act. I told this to Jeff. Jeff insisted and so did I. The guy never stopped calling. It was a campaign. "I know George's act," I would tell him, "with the hippy-dippy weatherman and the suit and the skinny tie. He's just not a Bitter End act." Jeff was relentless. "No, no, Paul, he's different now. He's got a beard, for Christ's sake." There was no resisting the appeal. I booked George for a trial week, and he sold the house out. I booked him for a ten-night Christmas–New Year show, and there was no looking back. A normal week, by the way, was fourteen shows, minimum. I remember giving George a check for over six thousand dollars at the end of the engagement. "Oh, wow," he said, "what a great way to start the New Year." Now I think George gets that per minute. George and the Bitter End have been connected ever since. When the Bitter End was under siege from its landlord in the late eighties and needed a legal defense fund, George, along with Robert Klein and Peter, Paul and Mary and Kris Kristofferson, came back and performed at the benefit. When the A&E television network did a *Biography* segment on George, they shot a lot of footage at the Bitter End.

The seventies is when the comedy scene first began to change for us. But then everything was changing for all the clubs in the Village. New York was no longer the strongest magnet for entertainment. Hollywood and California were taking over. Television moved West and was getting a little more hip. A lot of agents and opportunities moved West too. The Village clubs were still important, but we had a lot more competition. This was also when comedy clubs started opening up all over the country.

Throughout most of the sixties and early seventies there were only a few television shows that would play new music. The Smothers Brothers show was one example. Occasionally one of the late-night talk shows would play a band or a folksinger. There were *Shindig* and *Hullabaloo,* but they didn't last. If you wanted to hear folk or rock and roll, you had to come out to the clubs. Comedy was even worse on television because most of the new, groundbreaking comedy was either too political, antireligious, anti-Establishment, off-color, or all four. A lot of people watched acts like Richie Pryor on television and wondered what the big deal was. Richie used a lot of obscenity to great comic effect, but he was unable to do that on TV. I mean, of course, that he was unable to use obscenity in the early days of TV. Now, anything goes. But in the early seventies, if you wanted to hear dirty comics, you still had to go to the clubs. By 1972 some comedy acts like Cheech and Chong were actually featured headliners. I remember an agent calling me up one weekend to see who was playing, and I told him Cheech and Chong and Harry Chapin.

"But that's two headline acts on one bill," he said. I told him, "Sometimes you have to create magic." Cheech was a girl chaser, a good-time guy who was a lot closer to his stage persona than Chong was. Tommy Chong was a very intellectual kind of guy. I liked him a lot. Cheech used to say that "Tommy was the first kind of whatever it is he is that I'd ever seen."

It was around 1972 that a journeyman comedy trio was booked to play the Bitter End. The name of the group was Three's Company. They had some cute sketches, nothing outstanding, pleasant. There was a girl and two guys. One of the guys was named Bill Crystal. We got to like each other. He told me that when he was a kid, he had come to the Bitter End to see Woody Allen and he never forgot the experience. We had many odd things in common. Billy was young, but he knew a lot about the early jazz age. His dad was a jazz promoter and ran one of the best music stores in New York. Billy got to hang out a lot with his dad during Count Basie and Duke Ellington gigs. He knew Billie Holiday better than I did. She used to babysit him, for God's sakes. Nothing much happened for Three's Company, and I lost track of them for a while.

I didn't realize it at the time, but my days at the Bitter End, working for Fred, were numbered. Of course Fred's days of owning the Bitter End were numbered too. Until 1974 I was featuring Robert Klein and David Brenner quite a bit, but there were other acts as well. Don Imus came in one week during 1973. It was a circus. I mean literally a circus. Imus's crew came in and set up circus tents all over the club. I think they gave out popcorn and cotton candy. Imus was not a reformed partyer at that time, but most of his audience met him halfway, so it worked out all right. This was the time when he was creating all those characters like Billy Sol Hargus and the screaming chicken, which he still uses to this day. My favorite line by Don was when he said,

"I went to a party, and when I woke up, I had two teenage daughters."

Another comic who played quite often in the early seventies was Billy Braver, who has also gone off to work in television. The only thing I can remember about his act was a line about his childhood, "I was toilet trained at gunpoint."

In the meantime I got fired, bought the club next door, took over the lease of the Bitter End, and connected both places by punching a hole in the wall. I now called the club the Other End. The stage was moved to the other side of the old Bitter End and a stage was set up in the new Other End, and that's how we ran the club for a few years. If it sounds confusing, it was. It was at this time that Bill Crystal came back. He was calling himself Billy now and working on his own.

I don't think I ever worked as hard or rooted for an act as I did for Billy Crystal. He was being run by the Rollins and Joffe offices, but Jack and Charlie weren't involved in the day-to-day management. The actual nuts and bolts were handled by a guy named Buddy Morra. Billy was married with children by this time, and he needed the money. I played him every chance I could. I remember handling the contracts with Buddy or Jack Rollins. They always read: "This is to confirm that Billy Crystal will play the Bitter End for one week at three hundred fifty dollars a week, fourteen shows minimum, with the understanding that if business is good, you'll lay a couple of extra bucks on the kid." I always did. Billy was the leader of the next generation of comics. For Billy it was an incredible experience. Billy had the greatest rapport with his audience of any comic with the exception of Bill Cosby. And the work kept him alive and surviving through the lean years. For some reason it took a long time for the public and the industry to catch on to Billy. His first real break came when Howard Cosell stopped by the club one night and happened to see Billy's act and fell in love with him. Howard had a very short-lived variety show on television at that time. He was trying to be the new Ed Sullivan. The show didn't last, but it was on long enough for Billy to finally get some TV exposure. That got Billy noticed, but even then it was a struggle. He was supposed to be part of the original cast of *Saturday Night Live,* but it didn't work out, and he would have to bide his time with club dates until he finally got featured on Norman Lear's soap-opera satire *Soap,* where he played the first openly gay character on television. Everybody hated him in that role. The conservatives, the rabbis and ministers, and even the Gay Task Force sent him hate mail. Then Bitter End alumnus Joan Rivers cast him in one of her odd screen ventures. Somehow he played a man who was pregnant. He eventually got on *Saturday Night Live* and was a sensation, or as Billy would say, "I was mahhhh-velous."

My favorite Billy Crystal role was Morty the Mime in Tony Hendra's *This Is Spinal Tap.* During his nights at the Bitter End, I always made sure he opened for a good performer like Carly Simon or Jim Dawson so the room would be full. During the days Billy would go to tryouts and play basketball with Woody Allen. "I was guarding him," Billy told me, "and Woody said, 'Don't guard me too close, I tend to get nauseous.'" They played as a team and challenged bigger guys and beat them.

Billy was always dropping by the club to hear other acts. Around the time that Billy was playing, I was booking a lot of old-timers as well as new comics. We played Milt Kamen, who was Sid Caesar's stand-in on *Your Show of Shows.* Soupy Sales played for a week and, surprisingly, bombed. I liked Soupy, and the kids liked him too. Soupy always had a hip aspect to him, but when he played the club, I think he was trying too hard to be relevant. The audience was perfectly willing to sit through his silliness. It was what they came for. But Soupy was trying to change his style, and it didn't work. It was like going to see the Harlem Globetrotters and finding out that they weren't going to do the bucket-of-water trick. The audience was disappointed. Soupy was disappointed too, and at the end of the gig, when I tried to pay him what we had agreed to, he refused to take the money. "Just give me half," he said. "I'm not here to put you out of business." That took a lot of class.

Another seasoned comic was Pat Paulsen. Pat became famous as the house comic on the Smothers Brothers show, and especially when he ran for president in 1968. He used the TV show as a platform and would recite terse and wacky political editorials that are as funny today as they were then. But, like Soupy, he was trying to change. There comes a time in the career of any successful entertainer when the audience no longer expects originality. They want what they are used to. They only want to hear the performer's greatest hits. The artist almost has to shove any new stuff down the audience's collective throat. It's not easy. When Pat came to the club, he was trying to shed that dopey-politician image, and he couldn't. His new material was passé, and you could see that the audience wanted to hear him make an election speech. For Pat the problem was that the 1968 election was so close that it took days before anyone could admit that Nixon actually won the thing. Pat ran his campaign as a joke and actually wound up getting about 1 percent of the vote. Pat regretted it because he knew that those votes cast for him would have likely gone to Hubert Humphrey. But Pat appeared at the Bitter End during the Watergate hearings, and he was forced to go back to the old stuff. I remember him chiding the audience for laughing at his Nixon jokes. "That kind of attitude can only lead to investigations and convictions, and before long there'd be nobody left to run the government." He ran for president a few more times, but that was all you heard from him. He eventually settled in the California wine country and bottled his own Muscat. He died in 1997.

We ran a series of comics in the mid- to late seventies who became instantly successful, like Freddie Prinze. Freddie was just the sweetest guy in the world. He was crazy about Lenny Bruce and even dated Lenny's daughter Kitty for a while. Freddie played the club, in and out, in one week. About six months later he was starring on the hit television show *Chico and the Man.* About two years after that, he committed suicide.

Don Novello came in for a week as Father Guido Sarducci and kept returning until *Saturday Night Live* picked him up and made him a semiregular. The producers of *Saturday Night Live* were like baseball scouts. They checked out comedy acts all over the country. They had Tracy Newman's comedy workshop, the Groundlings, out on the West Coast. On the East Coast they had the Improv and the Village. *Saturday Night Live* actually started in the Village when Bitter End alumnus Tony Hendra wrote a play called *National Lampoon's Lemmings.* It premiered at my good friend Art D'Lugoff's club, the Village Gate. Rather than go with established stars, Tony hired a bunch of unknowns like Chevy Chase and John Belushi. He also hired Zal Yanowsky from the Lovin' Spoonful.

Gabriel Kaplan was a guy I could never figure out. First of all, he was a comedian who wasn't particularly funny. He was an actor who couldn't act. He wasn't a great-looking guy. He winds up having a career as a stand-up, starring in his own hit TV show, and then dropping off the face of the earth. He was okay. He would do a set and grab a couple of laughs. People would say, "Wasn't that great?" and I would say, "No." And they would say, "He's gonna be big." And they were right. One thing he did that was a riot was a drunken Ed Sullivan. Just the concept is funny.

It was a parlor gag. Gabe was at his best in a small room. And then I found out that most of the hysterical material that David Frye was doing during all those midnight drop-ins back in the seventies was written by Gabe. I mean during the Watergate era. And his show *Welcome Back, Kotter* was a huge hit, not least of all because one of the costars was John Travolta. And perhaps because the theme song was written by Bitter End alumnus John Sebastian. It was one of the few TV theme songs to go number one on the charts. Gabe was just a real likable schlubbo who was pretty funny every once in a while, and he turned highly unlikely material into an amazing career. He was the Sam Levinson of the seventies.

The only way to get two people to agree about Andy Kaufman is to call him a very strange bird. The common wisdom is to say that he was a genius. I thought there was something very traditional about Andy's humor. Traditional in a very untraditional way. A myth has grown up around him. Everybody is talking about him, telling stories about him, making movies about him. The actual performing Andy Kaufman could be a bit much. First of all, most of his bits were not original, but young people thought they were. For instance, he used to lip-synch over the *Mighty Mouse* cartoon theme song, coming in only on the part where the tenor sings, "Here I come to save the day." It was cute, but Jerry Van Dyke—that's Dick's brother—was doing that kind of thing years ago. Andy was a comic's comic. Liking Andy was very inside in the beginning. It became chic. But some people couldn't stand him. Robert Klein called it comedy through intimidation. Just stand there and scream until the audience laughs in self-defense.

Andy came to the club around 1972, and no one knew what to make of him. He told bad mother-in-law jokes, did Elvis impersonations, pretended he was a shy foreigner—in other words, a bad, demented Myron Cohen. But that was the whole point of his humor. It was supposed to be bad or goofy, and you basically had to laugh while you squirmed. The shy immigrant became Foreign Man and later Latka, the shy mechanic on *Taxi*. If it was Bill Dana doing his imitation Mexican, José Jiménez, the politically correct crowd would have gone through the roof. But I guess nobody gave a shit about Lithuanians back in the eighties.

In the beginning the audiences had no idea how to take Andy. His stage persona never implied that it was all a put-on. And quite often Andy would lose the audience. After Andy's appearances on *Saturday Night Live,* audiences finally got the joke, but Andy just got weirder and weirder. He seemed like he always consciously wanted to stay beyond his audience. If that's your goal, fine. Just don't walk around like a misunderstood savant. I could never tell whether his crazy act was really an act or not. Again, the general wisdom claims he was really crazy. Offstage he seemed pretty normal to me. He had a girlfriend who used to come down to the club all the time to watch him. He called her his little cloud. They were very sweet together. Like I said, in many ways Andy Kaufman was very traditional.

One of his big sponsors was Jay Leno. I think Jay may have even pushed Andy on me at some point. Maybe Jay identified with Latka. After all, Jay Leno used to work during the day as a Rolls-Royce mechanic. He would drive into the city and play the club for nothing. He desperately wanted to be on. I remember he would always come onstage with a little tape recorder that he would put on the piano. He would tape every one of his shows and go back home and study what worked and what didn't. The guys hanging around at that time, like David Brenner and Freddie Prinze, talked him into moving to New York. The problem with Jay was that he was one of those guys who could only survive as a stand-up. He wasn't going to get his own sitcom. He wasn't going to be a movie star. The only way to be a successful stand-up is to do your time. Work, work, work. That's what Jay did.

He worked the club for about four years off and on, and then one night he saw a mediocre comedy routine on the *Tonight Show* and said, "I'm better than that." Apparently he walked right out of his apartment, took a cab to the airport, and flew to Los Angeles. I understand Johnny Carson gave him a job.

When Steve Martin played the club, he was pretty scruffy. He had a beard and long, scraggly hair. His act was very similar to the kind of stuff he was famous for, the arrow through the head and the banjo and all that. But it didn't jibe with the way he looked. I know that David Brenner took him aside and gave him the best advice Steve Martin ever got. David told Steve to clean up, shave the beard, cut the hair, and dress up. It's an old lesson, but if a poor pushcart vendor falls down an open manhole, it's tragic. If a guy in a tuxedo falls down the same manhole, it's funny. That was when Steve adopted the white suit, etc.

Steve did his acts pretty religiously, like Woody Allen. He was not a great improvisational comic. His act was written, and he traveled with it for months and months, hardly ever varying from the script. The act he did at the Bitter End was the same act that eventually wound up on his classic comedy albums. When offers came in for television and movies, Steve jumped and never really returned to stand-up. Unlike Jay Leno, Steve saw himself more as a comic actor than a gag man.

When Jon Stewart came by the club in 1987, for his first-ever performance, he was calling himself Jonathan Liebowitz. At that time the comedy was being handled by my assistant, Wendy Wall, who was a funny lady in her own right. Jon went up on stage and bombed. I mean he bombed atomically. It was terrible to watch. By the time his set was over, Jon had had quite enough of show business. He said good-bye, vowing never to go near a stage again.

This was when Wendy came over to him and made Jon promise that he would return and try again a week later. Wendy was smarter than any audience, even a Bitter End audience. Besides, they may have all been tourists that evening. Jon came back and had a much better time of it. The encouragement that Wendy gave him was the turning point in his career. If you like *The Daily Show,* and who doesn't, you can thank Wendy and the Bitter End.

Tommy Chong once said, "What makes Cheech and me so dangerous is that we're harmless." That's a good way of looking at comics like Lenny Bruce and a lot of esoteric clowns like Paul Krassner, who founded the *Realist* and did radical-left stand-up on the side. Or Sandy Baron, who had great audience empathy and was the first comic to mix God, Zen, Sufi, Scientology, and Transcendental Meditation, only to find that his life still sucked. Or Darrow Igus, who is famous these days for staring in low-budget comic horror films like *The Horrible Doctor Bones.*

There were other comics, other clowns, but these were the best. The Bitter End, and clubs like it, kept a lot of good people working and surviving until the public finally caught on. And all the best comics played the small clubs like the Bitter End. The Bitter End comic alumni are the most influential hipsters and jokesters in the world.

Oh, did I mention Henny Youngman?

8

T<small>HE</small> O<small>THER</small> E<small>ND</small>

Be careful what you wish for, you just might get it.

— **Old French proverb**

N<small>INETEEN SEVENTY-FOUR WAS A PIVOTAL YEAR</small> for me. At first, I thought I had found a convenient opportunity to branch out on my own while still holding on to my job at the Bitter End. In 1970, Fred tried to institute another Bitter End on the West Coast. I went out to set up the business, hire the help, and book entertainment. Being in California was a gas, and it was fun hanging out with old friends from New York like Dion, Kris Kristofferson, Mickey Newbury, and others who were now spending as much time in L.A. as anywhere else. We were all young, energetic, horny, and a little wild. I got to meet and book artists who had yet to come to New York, like Al Jarreau, and we even recorded a Canadian heavy-metal band called Bush live from the Bitter End West. Going back and forth from New York to Los Angeles every month eventually became too much like work. There is only one rule when running a nightclub of any kind, and that is, the management must always be a physical presence. Everything else is secondary. Neither Fred nor I could always be there all the time, and so the usual problems inevitably ensued. The waitresses stole us blind. Booking errors or cancellations were never properly rectified. Trying to re-create a Greenwich Village club in L.A. was an oxymoron in any event. The Bitter End West was a kitten that should have been drowned. It finally folded, but it gave me ideas.

I went into partnership with two guys and bought the club next door to the Bitter End. Fred fired me, as I mentioned, and a few months later the landlord sort of fired Fred. "Oh, my God," I thought. "I wanted my own nightclub, now I have two of them." When Fred christened the L.A. club the Bitter End West, Tom Chapin laughed and said we blew it. "Paul, you should have gotten Fred to call it the Other End." I rarely let a good idea go unused, so with the landlord's permission I broke through the original wall and connected the two businesses and called the whole operation the Other End. For those of you who came to the club in the mid-seventies to early eighties, the red brick wall stage was now facing in the opposite direction. Like my other foray into California in the fifties, I was glad to be entrenched again in New York. When John Herald started playing the club in the late seventies, he recalled that just around 1974 he met Bobby Neuwirth, Steve Soles, and Rob Stoner at a recording session in L.A. A couple of years later these same guys walked into the Other End and had a songfest around the piano with Bob Dylan. This was the beginning of the Rolling Thunder Revue. John said, "I surely regret living on the West Coast and not being there. Otherwise I might have been on that tour." Alas. I now had a complete restaurant, bar, performance space, poolroom, everything you could want. And I was the boss.

As a club owner, you have your good days and bad days. I

dealt with nice people. I dealt with drunks. I dealt with all kinds of temperaments. People who didn't want to go home. Guys who left their tickets at home, and girls who wanted to sit in the first row. In the old days when we just sold soda and ice cream and the entertainment was generally folk music, the atmosphere had to be conducive to quiet, introspective music and poetry. We took the position that you were here to see a concert. That meant you had to shut up and listen. There was no argument about that. We had bouncers and managers who were tough cookies, and if anyone gave us any trouble, they were thrown out on the street. We had an enormous dishwasher who would stand in the doorway of the kitchen and fill the space. Assistant managers would go up to people making trouble and say, "I'm not your problem. That's your problem," and they would point to the guy in the doorway. We were young and rough, and the niceties didn't exist. The Other End was still laid back and relaxed, and the prices were reasonable. But sometimes the situation becomes more complicated, especially when you are supplying the booze.

One day I was in my little restaurant and in walks a Hell's Angel who was a little tipsy. I went over to him and introduced myself as the boss, and after a little conversation and a short drink, I told him I thought it would be a good idea if he went home, got some sleep. To my relief, that is what he decided to do. This guy was big, twice my size, with the beard and the patches and the death's-head on the back of the leather jacket. It was also long before the Hell's Angels reinvented themselves as a more socially acceptable bike club. He left, and I thought I had done a good deed. What I didn't realize was that he walked a few steps up the street and went back in the club through the other entrance.

In a matter of minutes, there was a great commotion in the club side of the Other End. An army of people started running to the back of the club en masse. Over a hundred otherwise normal people were pounding like a herd, screaming and yelling. Well, when you're the boss and something like that happens, you can't run in the opposite direction of where the trouble is. I still had no idea what was going on, because nobody wanted to stop and talk to me. When I got to the front of the club, there was a knife-wielding Hell's Angel. Even then, I wasn't exactly sure what had happened except there was a lot of turmoil and my doorman was lying on the ground moaning and clutching his chest.

My doorman was a nice, blonde midwestern guy whose wife also worked at the club as a waitress. The Hell's Angel went outside onto Bleecker Street still waving a pretty big knife, and my doorman looked like he was dead. I went outside and tried to calm this guy down and keep him busy until the cops came. At that time I kept my dog at the club, a big German shepherd named Max. Now Max is with me trying to go after the Hell's Angel, and I'm screaming at the dog because I don't want Max to get stabbed. The Hell's Angel must have sobered up in a hurry because he quickly took off down Sullivan Street as the ambulance arrived to take the doorman to St. Vincent's Hospital.

Now the real chaos began. The police came. There were hundreds of police. They were all over the place. I made myself scarce, because I really didn't witness the stabbing and I didn't want to get the club mixed up with the Hell's Angels. I figured there were enough witnesses without me having to testify. "If the cops ask for me," I told my bartender, "tell them I'm not here."

About an hour later, the police came back. They had a line-up, and no one could identify this particular guy. What a shock. All the cops knew about the Hell's Angels. Their clubhouse was on Fourth Street at that time, and they went down and arrested a bunch of them. The police station was also on Fourth Street, so it was easy for the cops to gather up the usual suspects.

The phone rang, and my bartender found me and told me that one of the Hell's Angels was on the phone. I wanted to kill him. "I told you not to tell anybody I was here." "I thought you were talking about the cops," he said. A voice on the phone said, "Paul, we need your help. You've got to come over here." I don't know these guys, but all of a sudden they know me. So off I go to the police station. I went in to the lieutenant on duty and said, "Listen, I've got to go in and talk to these guys. I want you to wait two minutes and then come in and get me out."

Sure enough, the Hell's Angels wanted me as a witness. I didn't see the guy stab my doorman, but as a witness I would have killed them. I could only identify one guy, and he was the guy with the knife. I walked in and said, "Fellows, I don't know what you want me to do. I've got a doorman bleeding to death up in St. Vincent's and some very pissed-off cops." In walks the lieutenant and says, "You're going to have to leave now." I thought, "Thank God."

The next day I got a call from Sandy Alexander, nice looking guy, ex-pro boxer, head of the Hell's Angels. He wanted to have a meeting with me. The only thing I could think of was Sandy making me an offer I couldn't refuse and my doorman bleeding to death. We met at a Chinese restaurant down the street from the club. Me, Sandy Alexander, and two other Hell's Angels were present. No notes were taken. I said, "Fellows, I don't know what you want me to do, but you can't put me in this position. If you cannot control your flock, that's your problem. I'm stuck, because if I lie and screw them, the police are going to come after me. I'm not interested in hurting the Hell's Angels, but my doorman got hurt and you're going to have to do something." Sandy said, "Paul, I understand. He shouldn't have done what he did." Then there was a pause and he said, "We'll take care of him." "All right," I said, "just don't put me in a position where I'm going to have to lie to the police."

What happened, as I found out later, was that my doorman, not seeing this guy was a Hell's Angel, saw him walk into the bar in a drunken state. With that, my doorman rightly said, "Hold it, you can't come in," and he touched him. I was to learn that you don't touch a Hell's Angel, you don't touch his woman, and you don't touch his bike. Any one of these three offenses is an open door for malice and death. Well, my doorman touched this guy and down he went.

Another day passed, and Jack the cop, our man on the beat, came up to me and said, "Paul, that kid of yours was the luckiest son of a gun I ever saw." "Why?" "That jerk used a knife with a four-inch blade, and it went right into him and missed every vital organ. All they had to do was sew him up." My doorman was released the same night. I didn't have a chance to talk to him, because the next day my doorman and his wife left for the Midwest. Not the least of their reasons was that they lived on Fourth Street too. They packed it in. They had seen quite enough of New York. This made my position a lot easier, since they didn't hang around to sue or claim damages. I don't know what happened to the Hell's Angel who stabbed my doorman, but I never saw him again, which was fine with me.

Now up to that point, the Hell's Angels never frequented the club or really had anything to do with that block of Bleecker Street. Suddenly they started coming around asking me if I needed any help, if they could do any favors for me. They started coming to the club. They'd call me up for reservations. They insisted on paying. It was a distinction I did not want. When we booked Robert Hunter, who was the lead writer for the Grateful Dead, they came by to make sure everything was okay. Lucky me.

Life went on. As the boss, I now had complete control of booking, and although we eased into loud rock and roll later on, I tried to keep the intimate feeling alive. This was a very happy time for me and my club. I finally got to book a lot of jazz acts. Some were up-and-comers like Grover Kemble and Za Zu Zaz. But I also booked more traditional acts like Jon Hendricks, Esther Satterfield, Esther Phillips, Stan Getz, and Stanley Turrentine. It was amusing and gratifying to see young audiences go wild for Stephane Grappelli, Les Paul, and Maxine Andrews. These were people I listened to as a kid. It was like living your life over again.

We played esoteric rock bands like Elephants Memory, who had the distinction of having Carly Simon as a lead vocalist for a short while in the early seventies and wound up backing John Lennon and Yoko Ono on a couple of albums. We also started to delve into the blues and had a string of pearls come and play like Mose Allison, James Cotton, Chris Rush, Jimmy Witherspoon, Otis Rush, Willie Dixon, and Taj Mahal. Taj Mahal was virtually unknown in New York at the time, and he received rave reviews that accelerated his career by light-years. Billy Crystal was now my house comic, augmented with Steve Martin, Biff Rose, and Christine Lavin, a very funny songwriter who was as good as a stand-up. Try listening to her album titled *Absolutely Live* and my favorite cut from it, "The Bitter End." We were really the ultimate nightclub.

This gave me great personal satisfaction because the Village had really taken a downturn. The neighborhood had gotten seedier and more dangerous. Drugs were no longer restricted to marijuana, and with harder drugs more pernicious characters started hanging out. A lot of the old clubs like the Gaslight, the Café Au Go Go, the Café Wha? and Folk City were either dying or dead. Business was tough for a lot of folks. I used this opportunity to book as many different kinds of acts as I could, and the response was gratifying. The stranger the better.

One of the most insane shows, part musician and part illusionist, was David Allen Coe. David was riding high on a string of hits made famous by other artists, most notably a song he wrote that was successfully covered by Johnny Paycheck called "Take This Job and Shove It." He was an unbelievably charismatic performer, and we hung out quite a bit. I knew he was special when he introduced me to both of his wives.

To begin one story and end another, I was in my house in Woodstock one day. It was Sunday morning. I got a call from David Allen Coe. I was very pleased that he called me. I said, "What are you doing?" He said, "I'm in Key West, fishing." I said, "That's nice." He said, "Yeah, I got my hand in the water, and I'm hoping to catch a fish." I said, "So I guess you want to play again at the Bitter End." He said, "Oh, no, no way." I was confused and asked him why. He said, "The last time I played for you, when we got back to Jersey, there was a bomb under my bus." I said, "You're kidding. Who would do that?" He said, "The Hell's Angels. I belong to a different motorcycle gang called the Outlaws, and the Angels are our biggest rivals. They've been after me for years. The last time I played Oakland, they torched my bus. I'll never play any gig west of Las Vegas anymore, and now it looks I won't be playing anything east of New Jersey." At that time dealing with the Hell's Angels was like dealing with the Mafia. Speaking of which . . .

Dealing with the mob was often a juggling act. Back in the fifties the Mafia was a potent and hydralike creature. There were rackets all over the city, and the mob had its hand in all of them. This was especially true if you were in the entertainment business. Nightclubs sold cigarettes and liquor; they needed to dispose of garbage; there was sex, drugs, and jazz, to coin a phrase.

And of course the mob kingpins had to entertain too. But the sixties confounded the mob in many respects. Here were night-clubs where a lot of the entertainment had the FBI on their back. Who needed that? The audience was highly critical of the United States government. This offended the Mafia. In their own weird way they loved America. Many local and federal laws allowed the mob to thrive. How could anyone be anti-American? There was plenty of sex in the sixties, but all the girls were giving it away for nothing, and the only beverages we sold were coffee and ice-cream sodas. Tommy Ryan or Tommy Eboli, it was the same guy, was running the rackets in the Village, which was near Little Italy. The only racket they could really force upon us was the cigarette concessions. They tried to make us use their cigarette machines. When we resisted, they couldn't go around assassinating us or burning down our clubs. The clubs all had apartments over them. One evening in the late sixties, I guess they had a meeting and decided on a unique plan of attack. They threw a stink bomb into the club. It was the nonalcoholic version of a drive-by shooting or an arson. It was the mob's answer to dealing with coffeehouses. It just made them look stupid, and they stopped. I must admit it was extremely potent, professional, if that's the word. The place stank for weeks. Managers and doormen had to throw their clothes away, and I think we closed down for a day or two. After that, they left us alone. By the time I took over in the mid-seventies, they were too busy shooting each other. Tommy Ryan, sadly, was one of the losers. Anyway, after the David Allen Coe story I started carrying a gun.

Of course, a gun doesn't help if someone pulls one on you first. I usually had the gun in the office drawer, but this night I left it in my shoulder holster. Two guys walked quietly upstairs into the office and stuck their guns in my back. They said, "We want you to show us the safe." Now the safe was downstairs in the club. And these guys knew it, so they must have done their homework. Before they took me down, one of the guys frisked me and got my gun. His partner said. "See, I told you." The guy who frisked me said, "You know, I could have shot you for that." I said, "How come you're entitled to wear a gun and I'm not?" He didn't like that at all. We went downstairs through the club. My friend Harold Leventhal and his wife were at one of the tables. He called me and said, "Paul, sit down and have a drink." I gave him a stone face and said, "Can I take a rain check?" and kept right on moving. Harold was a little shocked, but he didn't get it. So we went into the back room, and I turned to my partner, Dale Lind, who was, in his other life, a priest, and said, "Open the safe and give them the money." Dale started to turn the dial, and as he did, the fucking gun went off and put a hole in the wall. I said, "Great, I got a nervous burglar. Is this your first job?" Off they went with the money.

This was all small change compared to the running of the club and the challenge of keeping its prestige alive. The entertainment business is always in a state of flux. It does not matter what decade you are in or what the current rage is. Tomorrow it will all change, and you have to be ready. You are always in competition with someone, whether it's the latest rock emporium or a disco. If you are a club owner, inflation never evaporates.

I always understood that the Bitter End/Other End was in the Village and, because of that, you had to keep the entertainment fresh. Sometimes that meant going back to the old days. So in between Mongo Santamaria and Hugh Masekela, we would always bring back old friends like Mary Travers, Ramblin' Jack Elliott, Jerry Jeff Walker, and Tom Paxton. I remember bringing Bob Gibson back, for instance. Bob's drug use had finally caught up with him. He was busted in Cleveland in the late sixties and did jail time in Canada, where the cells are very cold.

He went off into the woods of upstate New York essentially to write his memoirs and fade away. By the late seventies it had become a little ridiculous imagining an aging junkie exhorting crowds of kids to sing along with him while he tried to pluck a banjo.

To everyone's surprise (or maybe not), Bob cleaned himself up and sprouted wings. He wanted to fly again, and I was happy to give him the runway. For a few memorable years I booked him and paired him with acts like Dave Van Ronk and Tom Paxton. Bob had become something of a legend, and the crowds came. His songs were as esoteric as ever. As Dave Van Ronk said at one of their concerts together, "If you wanted obvious things, you'd all be somewhere else."

We brought in Ben E. King to sold-out crowds, and that was fun for me because it revitalized that feeling that permeated the club when Stevie Wonder and Curtis Mayfield played. Ben did a lot of Drifters material. Doc Pomus showed up for one of the shows. Doc was an old Brill Building writer and composed "This Magic Moment" and "Save the Last Dance for Me." By the late seventies, he was confined to a wheelchair, and it was a very emotional reunion. Doc dropped by often after that. When Billy Vera played the club, he was doing a solo instead of his usual great act paired with Judy Clay. He was so happy to find a receptive venue that did not concentrate on hard rock, disco, or "wimpy singer-songwriters," as he called them. Doc Pomus came by to see him, and they met for the first time and stayed in touch over the years. Billy said that Doc was so kind and encouraging, and when Billy's record "At This Moment" went to number one on the charts, Doc wrote him a letter congratulating him. They even served together, later on, on the board of the Rhythm and Blues Foundation.

Other old friends like Jim Dawson played often. I remember

we booked John Phillips. John had failed to realize what practically everyone else in the music business who was John's age had eventually realized: speed kills. Jim was so excited about meeting and hearing John. When the show began, John was a mess. He played all right, but he wouldn't get off the stage and actually killed Jim's set. John kept it going for a few more years until his body finally said no. But that kind of self-abuse was happily becoming a rare occurrence.

We booked beautiful female vocalists like Morgana King. When Morgana started singing back in the fifties, she really wanted to be an actress. By 1974 she had appeared in the first two *Godfather* movies and established herself as a real star. By the late seventies she wanted to be a singer again and started releasing new albums. I have always been astonished at how versatile some performers are. Joni Mitchell and Bob Dylan are both very good painters. Allen Ginsberg was a wonderful musician. We played Rachel Faro for a week, and she offered the most beautiful new-wave music with Cuban, Caribbean, and African tones. I lost track of her career until I stumbled on a CD from Ashe Records only to find her name on it. She helped found the label and is now one of the most respected producers in the business. We also played one of the best cabaret singers around called Baby Jane Dexter. If you want to hear a cross between Sarah Vaughan and Bessie Smith, then Baby Jane is it. Come to think of it, if you want to hear a cross between Janis Joplin and Ma Rainey, then listen to an old friend named Maria Muldaur. What a voice! We played her often. Everyone knows her from "Midnight at the Oasis." It was a huge hit. She never repeated a performance like it again. She put the money in the bank and went back to singing the blues.

One thing we never changed was our support for up-and-coming artists. Probably the best to come along in the mid-seventies was Steve Forbert. Except for a Mississippi beginning, he had Bob Dylan's travel guide in his back pocket: a guitar, great songs, and a bus ticket to New York. He spent the days driving trucks, and at night he played the Other End. In the beginning I paid him fifty dollars a night. Within a year I was giving him twenty-five hundred dollars. I never saw anybody skyrocket so quickly.

I constantly had to deal with the press because for some reason the press does not feel like it is doing its job unless it slams somebody. I had to deal with reviewers coming in to see an act and dismissing both the artist and the club because they did not like the wine that was being served at the press party. I remember having to put a *Village Voice* writer in her place for knocking a Paul Williams concert because she seemed unable to accept the fact that Paul was short in stature. Paul Williams was a great talent and a ballsy guy who could hold his own in a recording studio, a record company, or hang gliding a couple of thousand feet above the earth. Paul is a good friend of another Bitter End alumnus, Jimmy Webb, who also likes aerodynamics, except Jimmy prefers hot-air balloons. Many novice reporters coming to the Bitter End for the first time seemed to expect a Vegas nightclub and always seemed to think they were creating a scoop by talking about the bathrooms or the church pews. In my time I took on representatives from *New York Magazine,* the *Voice,* the *Times,* and sundry other publications. I had no problem telling them all that the door to the club swings both ways.

Despite all the downsides of running a club, I could never have been happier. I was about to revitalize my relationship with Dylan. I was booking Andy Gibb, who was on the top of the world for a little while. I was producing concerts at Carnegie Hall and Alice Tully Hall with acts like Bill Withers, Dory Previn, and John Prine. Record companies were courting me again. They had begun to realize that the Other End was even more of a viable room than the Bitter End used to be. I quickly realized that you just did not open up a showcase room, you've got to earn a showcase room. I began to acquire the help and partnership that I would stick with through the millennium. I hired Kenny Gorka from a great eatery uptown on Ninety-first Street. Kenny used to be with the Critters and turned into the best talent finder I ever saw. If Kenny turned into my right-hand man, then Paul Rizzo became my left hand and treated my club as if it were his own.

In September of 1975 in an article in *Record World,* the reporter referred to me as the Mike Todd of Bleecker Street. I was flabbergasted, I was humbled, I was happy, and I was on top of the world.

9

Bob Dylan: The King and His Court

Any day above ground is a good day.

—Bob Dylan

BOB DYLAN AND GREENWICH VILLAGE and the Bitter End have been so inextricably connected for so long that it is almost impossible to describe one scene without the others. For Dylan, especially, the Village must have seemed like Paris in the 1920s if you were a budding writer. Around one corner was the White Horse Tavern, where Brendan Behan and the Clancy Brothers used to sing and hang out and where Dylan Thomas drank himself to death. Bobby Zimmerman started calling himself Bobby Dylan in honor of Dylan Thomas. Around another corner, on Patchen Street, lived e. e. cummings, who demolished all the rules of punctuation and grammar when he wrote his poetry. If you look on the back of Dylan's early albums, at the liner notes that he himself composed, you get that same iconoclastic style, and the influence of e. e. cummings is pretty obvious. The Village was where Pete Seeger lived and where Woody Guthrie used to hang out before he got sick. These were all the men that Dylan adopted as his spiritual fathers. And these people weren't vague, historical figures that lived centuries ago. You could run into most of them right on Bleecker Street. This was where they lived. For Dylan, coming to the Village from his birthplace in Hibbing, Minnesota, must have been like coming home.

In the beginning, Dylan was managed by Roy Silver. But Roy was only with Dylan for a short time. Roy worked for Albert Grossman in the beginning, and I think he was assigned to Dylan, but eventually Albert took over the management. In the early sixties, it seemed like everybody either wanted to perform or else manage a performer. If most of these guys hadn't supported each other and gone to each other's shows, there would have hardly been anybody in the audience.

I don't know if Albert Grossman had Dylan in the back of his mind when he created Peter, Paul and Mary, but it worked out great for everybody, especially Bob. They always did refer to Albert as "the Genius." When Peter, Paul and Mary got their start at the Bitter End and recorded all those early albums that just seemed to shoot instantly to number one, it was the first time that the average American got to hear a Bob Dylan song. All those tunes that PP&M covered, like "Blowin' in the Wind" and "The Times They Are A'Changin'," that became anthems for a lot of people and a lot of causes were heard long before Bob Dylan became a household name. In the beginning, I believe most people knew Bob Dylan, if they knew him at all, from other artists performing his material.

When Dylan first came to the Village, he was really a nobody from nowhere. He fooled everybody because he was so unique and of himself. It was as if he were dropped here from outer space. Bob Dylan, the Dylan that everybody thinks they know, was born in Greenwich Village. The first place he went to was Gerde's Folk City, which was run at that time by my old friend Mike Porco. Mike became another kind of father to Dylan, the kind that gives you money and feeds you. It was Mike who actually signed as next of kin so Dylan could get a cabaret license and perform legally in the clubs. Bob was only about nineteen when he first came to New York.

Jimmy Gavin, who later changed his name to Weston Gavin, was a singer, actor, comedian, and musician. He played the Bitter End once in a while, but everybody worked wherever they could. For a while he was Wavy Gravy's roommate over on Tenth Street. Jimmy was hosting the hootenanny at Gerde's during Dylan's first night in Greenwich Village. Jimmy recounted to me recently, "I remember him wearing a railroad cap. I wasn't particularly impressed with him. At the time, he was doing a very derivative Woody Guthrie imitation, but he managed to overcome it."

Tom Paxton also remembered that night. "Dave Van Ronk and I were sitting at Gerde's Folk City on a Monday night hootenanny when Bobby Dylan sang the first three songs that he ever sang in New York. They were three Woody Guthrie songs, and he had on his harmonica rack and a black corduroy cap, and you didn't have to be a genius to realize that here was someone special. Bob became, from day one, the hottest topic of gossip. You take an enigmatic personality and a first-rate talent and you have someone people talk about."

It was true. People couldn't get enough of Dylan, but nobody could have foreseen that he would ever make it as big as he did. In the beginning he was just one of a hundred or more unpolished guitarists singing protest songs in the basket houses. But there was a lot to learn playing the basket houses. One crazy place was called the Fat Black Pussycat.

They had a runway, and people would throw money up on

the stage, dimes, nickels. There were poor people in the audience for whom a dime was a lot of money. There were people onstage for whom a dime was a lot of money. Oscar Brand and Dave Van Ronk went down one night because Bobby Dylan was going to perform. They supported him. Dylan would eat dinner over at Oscar's house and sleep on Van Ronk's sofa. They liked him, but neither of them ever thought of the possibility of Dylan being a success.

In the early sixties there were two schools of folk music. One school was interpretive. You sang all the old songs, sea chanteys, wandering-rover songs, work songs, chain-gang songs. These singers perceived themselves as minstrels, and their duty was to revere the traditions and keep the old songs alive. The other school was more creative and wrote contemporary songs about hot topics or controversial problems of the day. Most performers were from the first school. Woody Guthrie was from the second. Pete Seeger could do both. Dylan stood firmly in the second school and placed his feet unapologetically into Woody's footprints. He was just like a little boy walking in the snow, following his dad's longer and deeper strides.

One of the biggest issues at that time was nuclear war. There were an awful lot of people who were scared to death. The United States was testing nuclear bombs in Pacific atolls and in the Nevada desert. People were building fallout shelters back then, and kids at school actually had to practice nuclear-war drills the way kids practice fire drills today. And then there was the Cuban missile crisis, which didn't help matters. The uneasiness was palpable.

Dylan used that whole intriguing and frightful tableau to create and perform all those early masterpieces. For Bob, the Village offered support, camaraderie, and escape from hunger. It also afforded him the give-and-take that artists need. When artists become successful and they rise out of the squalor that often inspires their first compositions, they end up in seclusion on the ritzy side of life. Which is great except that very often they can no longer maintain their initial success. Something is missing. Some gutsy fire gets extinguished, or they lose their street smarts and start playing from memory. Dylan was somebody who used all the elements that the Village had to offer, especially its spontaneity. And he was smart enough to return to the Village whenever he felt he was losing his edge.

He wrote "A Hard Rain's A'Gonna Fall" on Wavy Gravy's typewriter. Wavy, whose name at that time was Hugh Romney, was a leftover poet from the beat era. He was one of the first artists ever to perform at the Bitter End. Wavy's apartment at that time was right above the Gaslight on MacDougal Street. When Dylan finished typing out "A Hard Rain," he walked right downstairs into the Gaslight and played it. I think he sang it with Hamilton Camp backing him on the guitar. You can't get more spontaneous and contemporary than that.

When Dylan wrote "Blowin' in the Wind," he played it for Dave Van Ronk and a couple of friends up at Van Ronk's place. Dave told him, "Bobby, that is the dumbest fucking song I ever heard in my life. What wind? What answer? Let's get a little specific here." You could always say anything to Dylan because he'd never listen anyway. Van Ronk said, "So that was my opinion of the song for about three or four months. Then one day as I was walking across Washington Square Park, I heard a couple of young kids singing: 'How much wood could a woodchuck chuck If a woodchuck could chuck wood? The answer, my friend, Is blowing out your end, The answer is blowing out your end.' And I realized that if this song is being parodied after only a couple of months in circulation, and not even recorded, maybe I had better go back and listen to the fucking song again.

And I did, and I changed my mind."

Now these kids could have heard Dylan doing the song at one of the clubs, or they could have read it in publications like *Sing Out!* and *Broadside,* which were contemporary folk-song magazines put out by Pete Seeger and Sis Cunningham. These were little mimeographed sheets that published the first songs of people like Dylan and Phil Ochs. It was another facet of life in the Village that made it so inspiring for young artists.

Dylan also used to hang out at Chip Monck's basement apartment with Richard Alderson. Chip invented concert lighting at the Village Gate in the early sixties. Chip was the guy on the street that people would go to to light their shows. Because of Chip's talent and intuitive theatrical sense, the clubs became little jewel boxes for the artist rather that the artist being part of the wallpaper by the coffee machine. One of Chip's protégés was Jon Gibbs, who did the same thing at the Bitter End. Richard Alderson was Chip's counterpart in sound. Wavy Gravy found him making speakers for Leopold Stokowski. He eventually went on to tour with, and record for, Nina Simone. Richard was often at Chip's apartment and did a lot of recording. There are tapes somewhere of Dylan and Fred Neil and Hamilton Camp sitting around on weekends, passing guitars and singing and talking. Those are the real basement tapes you should listen to if anyone could get their hands on them.

There was a lot of technical talk, and consequently Dylan became keenly aware of all the mechanics of putting on a good show. Dylan was very good at taking little bits and pieces of other people's inventions and absorbing them and making them work for him. He took this great energy that was all round him and channeled it and made it his own. That's what genius does. Dylan, by the way, could be very funny on stage in a Chaplinesque manner. He had all these little bits of hand movements, a very kinetic style that was sort of based on Chaplin. People who saw him at the big arena shows later on, when he was a dot onstage, missed all that because, for awhile in 1971–72, he wasn't trying anymore. It was only when he played the smaller venues, when he used to open for John Lee Hooker, that's when the Chaplin character really came out of him, especially when he did all those crazy songs like "Talking Bear Mountain Picnic Massacre Blues" and "If I Had to Do It All Over Again, Babe, I'd Do It All Over You," which he wrote on a bet.

A bunch of people were sitting around the Kettle of Fish one afternoon, and, in between beers, somebody started rattling off joke song titles like "Take Back Your Heart, I Ordered Liver." According to Dave Van Ronk, "Somebody said, 'Bobby, I bet you couldn't write a song to *that* title, "If I Had to Do It . . .".'". So he came back a few days later with about six verses. Which I recorded. I think it was the first Dylan song to make it onto an album. It wasn't a great song but it was good enough. So I wanted to record it, and I still think it's pretty funny."

When folk music looked like it might get popular, the record companies were going crazy trying to sign artists. They were scared. They thought folk music might take off like rock and roll did in the fifties. They didn't understand the music or the artists, but every label seemed to want a stable of folk acts just in case. You didn't have to be brilliant to get a record deal, but the promotion people and the executives didn't know what they had. I don't think anybody bought Dylan's first album when it came out except a few enlightened souls like my friend Beverly Bentley.

Around the same time that Dylan's first album was released, I had a great apartment on Fifty-first Street and Second Avenue. It was a bachelor's apartment with a bedroom and a huge terrace. It had an above-ground swimming pool, and we used to hang out. Beverly Bentley lived down the block. She was shooting a movie called *Scent of Mystery,* and she was also on Broadway in a play called *The Heroine.* This was before she married Norman Mailer. She was hanging out with Miles Davis then. That's where I met Miles and got to know him. It was also the first time I was ever offered cocaine. It was a social scene. She would come to my house. I would go to hers. My house was the main hangout because of the pool. On the weekends all my friends, whom I called Fire Island rejects, would come over. They couldn't afford the train fare to the beach, so they went to my place.

Beverly came over one night with an album, a Bob Dylan album. She said, "You understand music; I want you to hear this guy." And she played Bob Dylan's first album. It had just been released, that day I think, on Columbia. She played it over and over and over. She said, "How'd'ya you like it?" I was a good friend. I said, "Give me some time to get into it."

I remember there was a black girl in the room. I can't remember her name or even why she was there, but there was a terrific fight. The black girl said, "Get that fucking piece of shit off the record player. I can't stand it." Beverly and the girl started fighting. Beverly kept saying, "Don't you understand this? You're not hearing something?" It was nuts. The black girl tried to take the album off the turntable and break it. But really most of the people at the party couldn't stand it. Beverly was the only one. This was sometime in 1962.

And then a week later Beverly said to me, "We've got to go down to the Village." I said, "Why?" She said, "I've got to meet this Bob Dylan." So we went down to Folk City that night, and the club was closed or Dylan was off, I don't know. But she was desperately seeking Bob Dylan. She was the first one with ears that were so rarefied that she could listen to that and say, "This is magic."

I still wasn't convinced until I found out it was John Hammond who signed him. So I had to look at him in a different light because I respected John Hammond. John used to come down to the Bitter End often. I knew him. I liked him. There was an internecine faction that tried to force him out of Columbia, but they couldn't. I don't think that first Dylan album helped, because I found out later that a lot of Columbia's sales staff said openly that the album was a piece of shit and wouldn't get behind it.

I don't know where Beverly met Norman Mailer. Probably at some party. She wanted to marry him very badly. She wanted me to meet him, but she said, "Be careful what you say." She invited me out to his house, and it must have been the Fourth of July, because we were sitting on the veranda watching the Statue of Liberty and the fireworks. It wasn't particularly pleasant. Mailer was pretty full of himself by that time. It was a long time since he had delivered copies of the *Village Voice*, which he helped found, to newsstands out of the backseat of his car. Sometimes I think Beverly would have been better off with Miles. I didn't see much of Beverly after she married Mailer, but she did introduce me to Dylan's music, which I shall never forget.

Dylan was never officially booked at the Bitter End. Bobby was very loyal to Mike Porco, and in the beginning, when he was an advertised performer doing a small club, it was usually at Folk City. Individual acts often became associated with one club or another. John Hammond Jr. always seemed to play the Café Au Go Go, the Lovin' Spoonful were usually at Nobody's, somebody else would be married to the Gaslight, and so on. The Bitter End had some great acts that were also pretty loyal. If you wanted to see Woody Allen or Bob Gibson or Theo Bikel, you would have to come to the Bitter End. For Dylan, the Bitter End was the place to go and listen and to take it all in. It was not where he worked but where he hung out.

Now the other great topic of debate at that time was civil rights. This was before Vietnam really became the issue. The first American casualty in Vietnam was just before Christmas in 1961, and about six months later there was a Greenwich Village peace committee formed to sponsor lectures on Vietnam. They eventually brought in guest lecturers like Bob Kerry, long before he became a senator, but it was not a burning issue yet. Civil rights, however, was on fire. Theo Bikel and Pete Seeger and others were very involved in the civil rights movement. There was always some kind of rally or benefit going on somewhere in the Village. And folk musicians were always on the bill. When I think of all the black jazzmen who played all over the Village back then, like Sonny Rollins, Roland Kirk, Charlie Mingus, James Moody, it was truly astonishing. But those guys lived in their own jazz world. It was a separate community. Every time there was a rally for the civil rights movement, the entertainment would always be a folksinger, who was usually white. I never could figure that out.

Theo Bikel used to play the club in the early sixties. He even did a live radio show on Sunday nights. Theo was very busy at the time. He was starring in *The Sound of Music* with Mary Martin, where he created the role of Captain Von Trapp. After the performance he would come down to the club to sing or hang out. Bobby Dylan would wander in and out, lugging his guitar with him, and he was often over at Theo's Greenwich Village apartment getting a bite to eat and playing his songs, which were very evocative. Theo was so involved in the civil rights movement that he used to go down South and get arrested, which was a dangerous pastime. He took Dylan aside one night and said, "Bobby, you shouldn't just write songs about this stuff.

You should experience it firsthand. I want you to come down South with me." But Dylan said he couldn't afford the fare. Just to call his bluff, Theo told Albert Grossman to buy Bobby a ticket and not tell him where it came from. He finally went down, but not until much later.

Another act that was very big at the time was the Tarriers. The Tarriers were also involved, like most of us were in one way or another, with the civil rights movement. It was hard for the Tarriers not to be, because they were one of the first, if not the first, interracial group. Two white guys, two black guys. One night during Theo's radio show, with Dylan in the audience, the Tarriers' spokesman and bassist, Marshall Brickman, was recounting from the stage a recent trip down South. "The four of us," he said, "were driving through Arkansas, about ten miles south of Little Rock. We were driving fast, very fast. It was a balmy summer evening. The air was thick and heavy with the scent of magnolias and honeysuckle and tar and feathers." Everybody laughed. But even with a free bus ticket, it was not the kind of experience that everybody wanted.

Curt Flood, the St. Louis Cardinals outfielder, said once that a person could be segregated in the backseat of a limousine. But Dylan wasn't like that. You didn't have to go down South to experience racism. The Village, after all, was not the idyllic neighborhood it sometimes gets credit for being. The Village could be crude and hateful. There was a lot going on back then, and it wasn't all flowers and love beads. There were working-class gangs, and the mob was always just around the corner.

When Len Chandler, a black folksinger who played all over the Village in the early sixties, almost died from a beating, it was Dylan who came to visit him in Bellevue Hospital. Len Chandler had been instrumental in bringing the Freedom Singers to New York. At the Newport Folk Festival in 1964, the Freedom Singers ended one of the evenings with a sing-along, and Peter, Paul and Mary, Pete Seeger, and Bob Dylan joined them. Because of Village regulars like Len Chandler and the Tarriers and people like Richie Pryor, Dylan understood the anger and frustration and the pain.

One of the original Tarriers, by the way, was Alan Arkin, before he became famous as an actor. Years later when Arkin and Bikel starred in the movie *The Russians Are Coming, the Russians Are Coming,* I heard that in between takes, the movie set was very often turned into the stage of the Bitter End as both actors sang folk songs to pass the time. People like Bikel, Arkin, and Leon Bibb were very good actors, and whenever they doubled as folksingers, their performances were tremendously effective because they could really act out a song. Lou Gossett Jr. did an act for years at the Village Gate with Felix Pappalardi on guitarron. It was quite an act. Dylan had seen and absorbed them all. And when these acts were impeccably staged by people like Jon Gibbs or Chip Monck or Richard Alderson and his protégés, it took on all the power of a theatrical experience. Of course, when Dylan picked an actor to imitate, he went with Charlie Chaplin. The point is that it was all part of his learning process. It was something that Dylan was keenly aware of.

Bob Dylan didn't play the little clubs for long. He was soon being booked into places like Town Hall and the big folk festivals. After the Beatles came out in 1964 and folk music began to get stale, Dylan did his great makeover from protest singer to rock star. When he played his famous electric set at the Newport Folk Festival in 1965, Pete Seeger got so outraged he tried to cut the power cables with an ax, and Theo Bikel wisely restrained him. That was when Dylan said, "Folk music is a bunch of fat people." But he kept his apartment in Greenwich Village, and he also kept the most important lesson folk music had to teach: the words are important.

By the late sixties Dylan was writing rock and roll songs with lyrics of such complexity and intensity that they frankly shocked people. He worked with Village-based bands like Paul Butterfield and the Blues Project, whenever Danny Kalb wasn't busy falling off rooftops, as well as musicians like Mike Bloomfield and Al Kooper. Dylan took rock and roll as his musical medium and wrote lyrics that you would expect to hear only in a folk song. That music spoke to a lot of people. Not only fans but other artists as well.

I really got to know Dylan well in the early seventies through Al Aronowitz, a rock critic for the *New York Post*. Al came running up to me on Bleecker Street one day as I was headed for the club. "Where have you been?" he said. It was early in the day. "I didn't know I had an appointment," I said. "Bob Dylan wants to come to the club." "So let him come. I'll give him a good table."

Now there was nothing stopping Dylan from dropping in by himself, but that was no longer the way Bob worked. That night Al brought Dylan, and I gave them my table. I believe Bunky and Jake were playing. They were one of Dylan's favorite acts. We all sat down, and before the performance started, I decided to make conversation. I knew Dylan had a house in Woodstock, so I said, "Bob, I just bought a house in Woodstock myself. How do you like it up there?" "Nice," said Dylan. I tried another angle. I started talking about food because I knew he loved our hamburgers. I asked him if the hamburgers were okay. "Nice," he said again. That was pretty much it. I let them enjoy the show.

About a week later I was outside the club checking on some posters, and Al comes running up frantically. "Paul, where have you been? I've been here since this morning." "Al, the club doesn't open until six o'clock at night. What can I do for you?" "Dylan wants to come by the club again." "So let him come," I said. "But he wants to make sure you'll be here." "Why?" I asked incredulously. "Because he likes you," said Al.

When Kris Kristofferson played for me back in the early seventies, he was not yet a big name as far as the public was concerned, but he was gathering quite a reputation. One day Kris said, "Let's go see Bob Dylan." Now I knew Dylan, of course, but you never knew how well you knew him. I may have had a drink or two that night. Kris had more than two, which was his way back then.

It was the apartment on MacDougal Street. We knocked, and Dylan's wife came to the door. We thought we were in a spy movie. We said, "We want to see Bob Dylan." Dylan's wife said, "Who wants to see Bob Dylan?" So Kris said, "Kris Kristofferson and Paul Colby." Well, she locked the door and went away. By now Kris and I were not sure what to do. About five minutes later she came back, unlocked the door, and we went inside.

Whenever I hung out with Kris, it was always a blast. The guitars would come out, and lots of drinks would follow. But not tonight. The conversation was a little bit about music, but Dylan's wife was there. I felt like we were old people all of a sudden. Out came the tea set. Here was Dylan, but he was very subdued. It was like intelligent people talking about the stock market. We all kept saying things like, "Oh, really?" and "Hmmm, interesting." It was completely nuts. I think Kris felt like screaming. At home with the Dylans. "Do come again. Don't forget to call before you come." That kind of thing. When Kris went on to do his cowboy movie about Billy the Kid, Dylan would star in it. But that night they didn't find each other. Dylan was at home with his wife that night.

Time moved on, and Dylan had gone off and done his country and western album including that duet with Johnny Cash. I remember seeing that first television appearance on the *Johnny Cash Show*. He did tours with the Band. People started talking about how his best stuff was behind him. By 1975, it was time for Dylan to come back to the Village, and that is just what he did.

When Patti Smith played the club in the summer of 1975, she had acquired cult status. A lot of people couldn't or wouldn't understand her, but the club was always packed with fanatics. That's when I remember Dylan coming back. Patti could be arrogant and blasé at the same time. The novelist Jerzy Kosinski came in to see her one night, and he had a copy of her book of poems called *Witt*. Kosinski got her to autograph it, but I don't think she ever knew who he was. When Kosinski spelled his first name for her so Patti wouldn't confuse it with the state, she misunderstood and wound up drawing a little map of Jersey anyway. He seemed satisfied, or resigned. Then Dylan came in. Patti knew who he was.

I think she was doing a cover version of a Rolling Stones song when he came in. They locked onto each other immediately. She said something to him from the stage like, "Don't think you can park your car next to my meter." The word was out. Dylan was back.

From that moment on, through July and August, Dylan was the hottest topic of conversation. Everybody wanted to know what he was doing back in the Village. What was up? I think he just wanted to hang out. He came to the club practically every night that summer.

Now by this time I had bought the club next door to the Bitter End, cut a hole in the wall, connected both rooms, and called the whole operation the Other End. For people hanging around from the beginning, it was still the Bitter End, except now it was huge. I was able to run a separate restaurant and even keep a pool table. When he first came by, I didn't realize it. He had walked in, and one of my bartenders said, "Oh, my God, that's Bob Dylan." Now you don't do that with Bob, and he walked out. I overheard the whole thing and ran out onto Bleecker Street after him. "Where are you going?" I said. "What are you doing here?" he said to me. I said, "This is my place." And he came back inside. I remember that first night, we were shooting pool together and my friend Billy Fields stopped by. Billy put his money on the table to shoot the winner. Bob beat me, and after they racked the balls, Billy started to play with Bob. Billy was in another world, and it wasn't until his second or third shot that he looked up and realized who he was playing with. It was one of the greatest double takes I ever saw. It was a special time for Bob. That is why he kept coming back. I made sure the scene was always relaxed and no one bothered him.

Now that Dylan was hanging around, I decided to turn July Fourth weekend into the First Annual Village Folk Festival, which it certainly was not, but hyperbole was always standard advertising procedure in the Village. After all, I had learned from a master. I know we had Jake and the Family Jewels on board and also Bunky and Jake, whom Dylan loved. It was a field day for the press. Bobby Neuwirth was hanging out, and so was Ramblin' Jack Elliott. Whenever Bunky and Jake or Ramblin' Jack got on stage, Dylan would join them and play and sing. It felt like hoot night again. Dylan sat down at the piano, and everybody onstage was singing "Will the Circle Be Unbroken?" Phil Ochs was hanging around getting drunk. Dylan was laughing, talking, and singing. He was so happy and relaxed. Bob looked at me and said, "This is like the old times." And it was. He was comfortable. He saw people he hadn't seen in years.

One night John Prine was playing. Bob got up, stood behind John Prine, and played the harmonica. Just little grace notes at first until he picked up the melody, and then he started to wail. John turned around when they finished and pointed his finger at Bob and said, "Dylan." That was it. There was a big round of applause. Now after the song he came back to my table. I stood up to let him in, and he sat next to me. Two girls were at the next table, and one of them said, "You're not really Bob Dylan, are you?" And I said, "No, but I am." With that, the one girl turns to the other and says, "See, I told you it wasn't really Bob Dylan." And the two of them walked out. The elusive Bob Dylan.

More and more people began stopping by the club. Cindy Bullens, Ronee Blakley, Allen Ginsberg, Eric Kaz, Logan English. Logan English was one of the first folkies to get onstage in the Village. I think Logan was playing around while Dylan was barely out of diapers. After one night of wine and tequila it seemed everybody wound up on stage. Eric Kaz sang "Love Has No Pride," the abstract painter Larry Poons got up and sang a song, Patti Smith recited some poem about King Faisal's nephew while Ramblin' Jack Elliott yodeled behind her. Dylan would just sit back in that dreamy way he had and smile. As Logan walked past him, Dylan said, "Is that you, Logan? I thought you were dead." Logan said, "I heard the same thing about you a couple of times." They both giggled. It was an incredible scene.

The only cloud over the space was Dylan's very justifiable fear that someone would tape-record him. He had a lot of new songs at that time like the songs about Joey Gallo and Hurricane Carter, and he wanted to break them in. This was another great aspect of the little Village clubs. You could introduce new material, try it out in front of a live audience, and work out any kinks. You could choose the best three verses out of half a dozen, tighten up a line here and there. But no professional would ever want his first drafts recorded. It also proved that Dylan needed some substance to write about. Vietnam was over, civil rights was no longer the big issue it was in the early sixties. Some artists saw the future as disco, but not Bob Dylan. He was writing a song to try to free a black convict who he thought got railroaded.

On this particular night, it was getting late and the place was closing up, but nobody would leave. Dylan told me that he wanted to get onstage so bad he could taste it, but he was worried. "These are new songs. I just want to make sure I'm not recorded." I said, "All you have to do is let me know." Now I don't know if Dylan saw something that made him suspicious or not, but sure enough, there was a girl at one of the back tables with a tape recorder and her pocketbook open.

I went to her and said, "You're involved in a happening here. This is a very special scene you're in. People would give their right arm to be here." I told her to shut the thing off, and I took the tape recorder and told her I would give it back when she left. Charlie Rothchild was standing by the bar rail. Charlie was a producer and worked with Allen Ginsberg and Judy Collins. He said, "Paul, they've got another tape recorder." Then I blew my top. I got so mad I pulled the tape out of the machine, and Charlie Rothchild started pulling the tape out of the reel. This girl's boyfriend said, "Hey, I got other stuff on there."

I said, "I don't give a fuck!" I had a glass of wine in my hand. He tried to say something else, and I threw the wine in his face. Then I threw him and his girlfriend out of the club. That's when Bobby Neuwirth came over to me and said, "Paul, Bob Dylan and I want to do a tour." I said, "Great." He said, "Do you think you could do it?" "Sure," I said. I had no idea how to do a tour, but I figured I could get people, organize them. I felt I could do anything. No big deal. That was the beginning of the Rolling Thunder Revue.

As we talked about it a little more, I said, "Look, you guys are having such a great time here. Musicians need to get back to their roots, to the small clubs. You're always talking about how sick you are of the concert scene. Let's not do arenas. Let's do the small, intimate two- or three-thousand-seat theaters."

Both Dylan and Neuwirth said, "Great idea." Everybody in the room that night was titillated. It was as if they were all somehow involved in the tour. Jack Elliott was having a large tequila. Bob called to him and said, "Hey Jack, you want to go on tour?" Jack said, "Sure." A couple of weeks later I saw Jack, and I said, "So are you going on tour with Bob? "and he said, "Hell, no. I thought they were all drunk."

In walks Roger McGuinn from the Byrds. "Roger, come here." Roger goes over and sits next to Bob, and the next thing I know, McGuinn is on the tour. Ronee Blakley was in the room. She was on the tour. Everybody was getting an invite. "We're having a party, come along." I was going to be the tour director. Finally the police came and told everybody to go home. It must have been five in the morning when we finally left. Then they actually got serious, and they started to rehearse at the Bitter End practically every night after the regular shows were over. Ginsberg, McGuinn, Blakley; I think Joan Baez got involved around this time. Joan was never really of the Village. She was from the upper crust of Massachusetts, but if Dylan was involved, she would deign to hang out with the proles. I think she was always a little bit miffed that she and Dylan never created some kind of dynastic marriage. Here the guy is married with five kids, but she always considered herself the queen, and so it was only natural that she should be bonded to the king. Everybody wants to be the One.

Dylan and I went out a couple of times. He was always discreet. One girl came to me and said, "You know, I have to talk to you. You seem to know Bob Dylan. Well, I had an affair with him a couple of weeks ago. He said he cared about me, but I haven't heard from him." "Did you enjoy yourself?" I asked. She said, "Yes." I said, "Well, think of it as a fond memory." They're all the same. She had his body, now she wanted his brain.

The rehearsals went on for weeks, and they were always late-night affairs. I went home one night to Jersey at about four in the morning. Someone called me an hour later and said, "The cops are at the door. What'll we do?" I said, "Keep the doors locked and pretend you're not there."

The regular shows for the public would end around 2:00 A.M. Then everybody would start drifting in to rehearse. The audience would leave as the cast members and friends would be coming in. One night around 3:00 A.M. I'm listening to them rehearse, and the telephone rings. It was Eric Andersen calling from Woodstock. When he heard the music in the background, he said, "What the hell is going on there?" So I told him Dylan was there with everybody and they were all rehearsing for a tour. "Wow," said Eric, "It sounds great. How long will it be going on?" "What do you mean?" I asked. He said, "If I drive down right now, will it still be going on when I get there?" I said, "Drive slow. They'll be here for two more weeks."

Phil Ochs was around a lot then too. Bob thought I was being cruel to Phil Ochs because I was short with him. Phil was driving me crazy. He was drinking heavily, he was a mess, and I had told him that I would buy him no more booze. I didn't want to encourage him. Dylan told me to buy him a bottle of wine, which I did. I couldn't sit Bob down and explain to him that Phil was going off his rocker. Phil would come around drunk and bad-mouth Dylan. Then when Bobby would show up, they would be best buddies again, and Phil would have his arm around Bob. This happened a lot.

Many of Dylan's contemporaries had a love-hate relationship with him. They all started in the business around the same time, and in the beginning everybody was on an equal footing. I think the feeling was, "Sure, Bobby's good, but he's no better than I am. Why don't people buy my albums anymore? How come I'm not making a million dollars?" Dylan inspired a lot of jealousy, but very few people would ever say so to his face. In fact, just the opposite happened. There was always that one big question. Why him and not me? There's an easy answer to that, and everybody knows what it is. Some people accepted it, and others, like Phil, became self-destructive.

When the Rolling Thunder Revue finally started, I was pushed out of handling the tour. It would have been difficult in any event, but I think I could have handled it as well as it eventually was done. In the beginning, I saw about four or five shows. I was something of a fixture because I guess they felt indebted to me, or guilty, I don't know. I went up to Plymouth, Mass., to see the first concert, which was done in a church, about a thousand people, just as I had suggested. Everyone on the tour was staying at the local inn, and I was the only outsider allowed in. The press had to stay in Plymouth. Bob invited me up onstage to sing for the finale. I got to watch all the intrigue up there. All the girls trying to go to bed with Bob Dylan.

The tour was eventually given over to Barry Imhoff. Bob Dylan's best friend Lou Kemp was also around a lot. Barry and Kemp were the leaders of the pack. The Rolling Thunder Revue became the last great tour that Dylan did. It was a great success because they really did try to keep that original feeling to it, except that by the end it had more or less reverted back to the big venues. The tour was going to end at Madison Square Garden. I remember running into Kemp just before the Garden show, and I told him, "I've seen four or five of these things already. I'm not going to the Garden." Kemp said, "Yes, you are." I said, "No, I'm not. I've seen enough of him." He said, "I'll bet you." I said, "What do you want to bet?" He said, "A high-priced hooker." When in doubt, bet a high-priced hooker. So we bet a high-priced hooker and I lost. I went to the Garden show. The reason I went was that Hurricane Carter was going to be there. They had a lot of celebrities, and they made a big deal out of it. The next time Kemp comes to New York, I intend to pay him off, except that these days, he may want to change the stakes.

That was the last time I saw Dylan. Why he never came around again I don't know. When someone asked me why Dylan was back in the Village and why he kept coming to the club, I said, "Because he likes my hamburgers." But that was another aspect of Dylan. He was fickle. He could cut you off as fast as he could embrace you. I don't think it was spite. It was simply time to make a change. Time to go. When Jackson Browne played the club, he wanted to meet Dylan. I took Dylan in to see him. They talked. Jackson took the stage. After the first two songs Dylan got up and left. Poor Jackson said, "There goes my career." But not so. Dylan's disappearances were as quixotic as his appearances. He was a guy you simply enjoyed but could never get close to. Many people think they are close to him and they are—until he disappears.

The last time I heard that Bob had stopped by was February in 1992. He had apparently gone to the Beacon Theater to see Neil Young, and after the show both Neil and Bob went to the club to hear David Bromberg do a set. I wasn't there. When his new album came out in the late nineties, I got the feeling that it was missing that edge. I think Dylan needs to hang out in the Village again and stop by the club. I think it's about time for that. When he got sick a few years ago, I got calls from all the newspapers. "Why call me?" I thought. Then I suddenly realized that Folk City is gone. The Au Go Go is gone. Nobody's is gone. The Gaslight is gone. Art D'Lugoff and Manny Roth and Mike Porco are all gone. I'm the last one left. The Bitter End and me.

I told the newspapers, "I'm sorry he's sick, but I'm eighty years old and I still enjoy working. What do you want me to say? He doesn't call me. I hope he feels better."

10

RAISING THE BAR

*If you don't fail now and again, it's a sign
you're playing it safe.*

—Woody Allen

TIM BUCKLEY ONCE TOLD ME that rock and roll had to be loud because in today's world it was the only way you could get people to listen to you. I'm sure that was correct back in 1972 when he played for me, but it doesn't seem true now. Maybe that's because rock and roll has lost some of its edge. There is a good reason for that. Rock and roll always had many myths surrounding it. The most persistent myth was the one that categorized rock and roll as rebellious and anti-Establishment. Forget the fact that it was a myth to begin with . . . but now? Rock and roll is so much a part of the Establishment these days that it is difficult to keep up the pretense. Many rap artists and bands like Limp Bizkit can scream obscenities all they want, but nobody's shocked anymore. These days rock and roll *is* the Establishment. It's put on Muzak and played in elevators and dentist offices. Rock is sung at inaugurations, it's played in churches and heard on TV commercials to help sell everything from minivans to dog food. Even Rush Limbaugh introduces his radio show with rock and roll. What's a poor rebellious rock band to do?

I think that the best bands will go back to basics and concentrate on making good music and being entertaining. If you don't have that, you don't have anything. There is little need to attack the Establishment anymore. Like Pogo used to say, "We have met the enemy and he is us." One lesson that new bands must learn quickly is that the "kick 'em in the balls" attitude of the old rockers was mostly hype. When the old bands became successful and played the huge arenas, there were a lot of bad performances and some piggish behavior onstage and off. When these bands played the Bitter End, they couldn't get away with that stuff. There was nothing separating the musicians from the audiences, and if the musicians had gotten rank and abusive onstage, the audiences would have killed them. Most musicians sense this and know that if they want to be successful, they are going to have to concentrate on what this business is all about— entertainment.

Of course when there was an "Establishment," a lot of strange things did happen, especially in the Village. There was a slight problem, but then there always was a slight problem, with the authorities. I don't mean the working cops on the beat. We always had good relationships with them. I mean the feds. Anybody who supported civil rights or railed against nuclear war and Vietnam was sure to get investigated. Right from the start, we had government informants lurking about trying to hunt down insurgents or people like Lenny Bruce. As rock and roll started becoming the music of choice for most of our audiences, the number of "observers" in and around the Village increased. Rock and roll also had an affiliation with drugs and a tendency to call attention to itself. The attitude was "Catch us if you can."

My first real foray into rock and roll was when I booked the Everly Brothers back in 1969. While people like Tim Rose, Mama Cass, and the Chapin Brothers had been slowly sneaking in a rock and roll sound with a folk message, Don and Phil were old-style rockers. They either sang about being in love or not being in love, and that was it. We always had home-based pop music acts like Spanky and Our Gang and the Nitty Gritty Dirt Band. Spanky McFarlane would go on to replace Cass Elliot in those numerously attempted revivals of the Mamas and the Papas, and the Nitty Gritty had a huge hit with Jerry Jeff Walker's "Mr. Bojangles." There were always acts that skirted the issue of classification, like Dr. West's Medicine Show and Junk Band. This was a crazy jug band run by Norman Greenbaum, who had a respectable hit, years later, with "Spirit in the Sky," a Jewish version of a Jesus love song. The most popular song the Medicine Show did at the club, however, became a minor underground druggie classic called "How Lew Sin Ate." There were often men in dark suits checking out the Medicine Show, and they weren't from the record industry. Jim Dawson remembers performing at rallies, being photographed, and then being audited by the taxmen. Bill Deseta, who used to manage the club before me, remembers a party with Spanky and Our Gang, of all groups. "There was a party in somebody's loft, and the bass player was talking about killing President Johnson. There was a Secret Service guy at the party and they busted him." I can't verify whether or not Oz Bach was the bass player in question because, sadly, he died a few years ago, but he was a hilarious free spirit. It just might have been something he would have pulled. Oz spent a career backing up people like Josh White, Fred Neil, Tom Paxton, Odetta, Bob Gibson, Gordon Lightfoot, Cass Elliot, David Clayton-Thomas, and David Steinberg. And this was before he met Spanky. A lot of people don't remember that Spanky and Our Gang actually had one of their songs banned on AM radio for being too political. If Spanky and Our Gang could get into political trouble, anything is possible.

I was in touch recently with the southern-born rocker Sam Neely, who played for me in 1972. When I asked him about his memories, he wrote back: "Seems we were taken care of during our stay in New York. Every night at the show there were five big guys with black suits sitting at one of the tables. Stood out like a sore thumb. Everywhere we went in New York, they were right around the corner." During rallies and outdoor concerts there were always guys in suits taking lots of photos. It was just an unpleasant fact. I'd like to think there's a file on me somewhere.

Anyway, back in the late sixties and early seventies as acts like Van Morrison, Chuck Berry, and Bill Haley began to draw heavily, I knew that the business was changing again. If the Bitter End was going to survive, it was going to have to change too. I desperately wanted to get a liquor license. Every improvement brings its own kind of trouble, but it just seemed ridiculous to invite adults into the club to entertain them and only serve ice-cream sodas. That eventually occurred in 1974. when I finally took over the club. By that time the Tin Angel was no longer in operation. I would like to take a moment to blow taps for the Tin Angel.

While the Bitter End is known all over the world, the Tin Angel was a local secret. Except for Joni Mitchell's song by the same name, I doubt if anyone outside of New York would remember it. The Tin Angel was started by Fred Weintraub and Bill Deseta. In the early days Fred or whoever was running the Bitter End would travel a block or two to eat dinner. Somebody would always be running around the Village trying to find them because a problem had arisen. There was always some problem or other. Fred wanted a restaurant nearby, so he started his own. Eventually none of us could get a seat in our own restaurant. We hadn't realized that because we were there, the acts would come up to eat too. The acts would be followed by every other person who wanted to be part of the scene. We also had the most gorgeous waitresses in the city. Pretty soon the Tin Angel became a bigger madhouse then the club. It was basic food, low prices, and you got a lot for your money. Anyone who ever had a burger at the Tin Angel can attest that they were the best in the city. What they probably didn't know was that the burgers were created by a mad chef who used ox hearts as part of the recipe. This guy actually cooked at night and sold dildos as his day job. After the Tin Angel closed and I bought the restaurant next door, we finally had a bar, good food, and a nightclub. Now we were really ready for rock and roll.

One of the first things we did was create a soundboard and an amplification system that could work effectively in a confined space. The Bitter End has a very low ceiling and a wide expanse of wall, which is mostly brick. It took technical know-how to do it right. This was all new to me, but I felt I owed it to the artist. After that, it was up to the artist. I decided to jump right into the water. Rock clubs were popping up all over the place, and rock bands were finding usable venues at college campuses, sporting arenas, and places like Bill Graham's Fillmore East, and I wanted to be part of the mix.

In the beginning it was tough. Aside from the excitement and challenge of trying to change a folk club into a nightclub that only sells ice-cream sodas, my main concern was getting six or seven musicians playing high-voltage rock to make it sound understandable to an audience sitting three feet away. Another problem was informing the press about the changeover. The folk-club label was hard to alter. For years I remember calling critics from *Rolling Stone* and the *Village Voice* and complaining that they kept calling the Bitter End a folk club. "Is Stevie Wonder folk? Is Curtis Mayfield folk? Is Jackson Browne folk?" "You know, you're right," they would say. "What should we call you?" "Call me a nightclub." It took a lot of convincing. In spite of the difficulties, I was committed to keeping rock and roll at the Bitter End. I also realized that, for the good of the club, I should not allow myself to get typecast again. I wanted the Bitter End to become the premier nightclub in New York City. Why not?

I'm not sure if anyone remembers a band called Rhinoceros, but back in 1969 they were highly touted, and expectations for them were huge. Rhinoceros was the brainchild of my friend Paul Rothchild, who worked for Elektra Records. Paul was a superstar in his own right and was making a big name and a fortune for himself by producing the Doors. When he needed a follow-up project, he was determined to make it a bigger hit than the Doors. He got the idea to create what he called a "supergroup." He would go about, glom players from other bands, and make a whole new organization. At first blush it sounded like a brilliant idea. Maybe if he had gotten Jimi Hendrix and John Lennon and Eric Clapton to form a band, it might have worked. But the guys in Rhinoceros were not exactly superstars to begin with. He took a guitar player from Buffalo Springfield, another one from Iron Butterfly, a drummer from the Mothers of Invention, a keyboard player from the Electric Flag, etc. and called them Rhinoceros. If he had only added a solo horn player, it would have been funny.

They were formed in California and made an album that didn't go anywhere. By 1968 they had relocated to the East Coast. One of the problems about the band was this tag, supergroup. Paul Rothchild and Elektra Records kept promoting them that way, and although the public was interested, a lot of other musicians resented it. The feeling was, "Hey, what are we, chopped liver? How do these guys become a supergroup when their record is number 115 on the charts and our record is in the top 10?"

I must admit that when they played the club, Rhinoceros packed the house. It was one of the best-attended shows we ever put on, but the band drove me crazy. The sound was way too loud. I told them that part of stagecraft is to realize where you are playing. They wouldn't listen. Maybe they couldn't hear. The sound was so ear-splittingly loud that I believe they actually irritated the audience. I was worried because I didn't want the public to blame the Bitter End for the bad sound. All I can say is that they didn't listen to me and Rhinoceros is a memory.

We still played folk music acts like Tom Paxton, Jim and Jean, David Ackles, and some others, but pure folk music was becoming outdated. After Bob Dylan's jam with the Butterfield Blues Band at the 1965 Newport Folk Festival, even traditionalists were arming themselves with drums and electric guitars. Arlo Guthrie was a perfect example. We were one of the first clubs to introduce Arlo Guthrie to New York audiences. Arlo was fresh off his success with *Alice's Restaurant* and his great success at the Newport Folk Festival. Arlo came to the club at the end of 1967 and played a number of times during the following year. He recorded his follow-up album to *Alice's Restaurant* at the Bitter End. The album made it to the top 100 on the charts. Actually it made it to 100 exactly. It's not the best, but it's better than 101. To this day Arlo jokes that it is the worst album he ever made. But the point was that here was the son of Woody Guthrie, someone who grew up hanging out with Pete Seeger and the Weavers, and even Arlo was moving toward rock and roll.

Joni Mitchell played for me around 1968 and did very well.

Everyone loved Joni, and I was very keen on giving her good opening acts. I played her behind Bunky and Jake, who were one of Bob Dylan's favorite acts. Sometimes Bob came in when Bunky and Jake were playing and left before the headliner got on, but not when Joni was the star. One of Joni's opening acts was Neil Young. The record label was very insistent that I play him. Back then, when a record company had great faith in an act that had not yet caught on with the public, they often used the Bitter End to keep their stars eating. When it was finally Neil's turn to headline, the record label wanted me to play him at five hundred dollars a week, which was a lot of money in those days. I remember telling Neil's agent that he wasn't worth it. Nobody outside of the business and some diehard Buffalo Springfield fans knew who he was. I kept getting pestered, but I insisted that Neil wouldn't even draw flies. It wasn't that I had anything against Neil, but I felt it was too much money. "We can't give him anything less than five hundred dollars, Paul. It would destroy his confidence."

Finally we worked out a deal. Neil's contract read in part: "There are to be two shows nightly except Friday and Saturday when there will be three shows. (Tuesdays off.) The total price of this engagement will be one thousand dollars or five hundred dollars per week." What Neil didn't know, and what he still doesn't know, was that the record label and I came to an agreement ourselves. I kicked in three hundred dollars and the label kicked in the other two hundred. They didn't want to hurt Neil's feelings. I had to take out an ad that read "Neil Young (formerly of the Buffalo Springfield)," but it didn't help. He still didn't fill the house. I thought the only way to put people in the seats for him was to have him front for somebody that could draw well, and on one occasion I picked Joni Mitchell. Early in 1969 I felt that Neil was going to be such a force that I let him headline.

There was a lot more excitement building around him by then, but he still couldn't fill the room.

Right in the middle of August 1969, the Woodstock Music and Art Fair was all over the newspapers and television. Not only did Neil Young become a household name, but so did a lot of other people. A big chunk of the Woodstock talent pool had been hustling around the Village for years. Arlo Guthrie, Tim Hardin, Richie Havens, John Sebastian, Melanie, Jimi Hendrix, Janis Joplin, Wavy Gravy, Paul Butterfield, Joni Mitchell, and Blood, Sweat and Tears. I remember just after Woodstock, Jake Holmes ran into David Clayton-Thomas upstairs at the Tin Angel. David took Al Kooper's place as lead singer for Blood, Sweat and Tears. David called Jake over to his table and said, "Jake, listen to this. It's one of our new songs." David started singing, 'What goes up . . . must come down. Spinning Wheel . . . got to go 'round." Jake said, "That's the dopiest song I ever heard." "No, it's not," said David, "It's gonna be great." I agreed with Jake. What did we know? I think "Spinning Wheel" was number one on the charts for a month. My instincts about rock and roll were weak, and I decided I was going to have to take the time to really understand rock as an art form.

I played Neil Young, Joni Mitchell, and others for Elliot Roberts, who was in business with Dave Geffen. In those days I would get options on replays. I would play an act for five hundred dollars with the option of playing the act again within a year for seven fifty and then perhaps again for twelve hundred. If the act attained very high star status, I would play them in concert at places like Carnegie Hall. After Joni Mitchell played, Elliot Roberts wanted to buy my option out. Joni was breaking out, and they bought out the option, which, in a word, stinks. Clubs like the Bitter End take great chances every week on one act or another. The prestige of having the artist return to play the club after they become well known is an intangible benefit that can't be translated in terms of money. Now they were trying to pull the same trick with Neil.

One day while I was at home, I got a call from Dave Geffen. "Why can't I get a fucking act in your club?" "Why should I put your acts in my club? I play them when they're nobodies and then when they start making it, you give the acts to other promoters. You never honor the options. I can't make any money." "I'm asking you again," said Geffen, "What do I have to do to get Jackson Browne in your club?" I said, "Simple, repeat after me: I will honor my options." "Okay, you shit, I'll honor the options. Now put in Jackson Browne." David Geffen was such a pleasure to do business with. I said, "Fine, send him around." Jackson Browne played once, made a big splash, and Geffen never let him play again.

David Geffen wasn't the only one. James Taylor was another act that didn't sell out. James was an act that I believed in and wanted badly. Someone sent me his first album and I loved it. What really impressed me was that Apple Records was his label. Peter Asher was handling his management and I figured if the Beatles were behind him, then this must be magic. I was right, but it took a little longer for the public to catch on. But here I was again with the options. James plays and fails to sell out, but the press is bubbling over about him. But now James gets into a motorcycle accident and is incapacitated for some months. Of course the options come due. How can you pick up the option on a guy who can't get out of bed? I couldn't pick up the option and make James Taylor get out of bed to honor the contract. When he got better, they wouldn't bring him back. It had nothing to do with James. It was the agent.

To show you how crazy things could get, I'll never forget when Hal Ray from the William Morris Agency wanted me to put his new artist, Jimmy Spheeris, into the club as an opening act for a Christmas-week show. Hal represented Jimmy and Ten Wheel Drive, who were already on the bill as headliners. Jerry Schoenbaum, who was head of Polydor Records, wanted the opening act. Polydor was Ten Wheel Drive's record label, and he spent a lot of money promoting the show. Hal Ray was insistent. "If you don't put Jimmy Spheeris in the opening spot, I'm going to pull Ten Wheel Drive." The show was only a week away. "Hal," I said, "I can't do that. Jerry's spent a lot of money on publicity. I have to give him the opening act." Dead silence. "Did you hear what I said? Put Jimmy on the bill or I'll pull Ten Wheel Drive." "Hal, I'm sorry but I can't do that. You'll have to pull the act." More silence. "You son of a bitch. You'd really let me pull Ten Wheel Drive, wouldn't you? All right, forget about it."

A few years ago an agent came into the club and was surprised to see me. "Wow," he said, "you're still here. How did you do it?" I said, "I didn't let you guys fuck me." He just stood there with his mouth open.

There's an old joke about an agent sitting in a waiting room and suddenly a hole appears in the floor, fire and smoke belch up, and the devil stands before him. The devil says, "I'll give you anything you want. Money, fancy cars, a big house, fast women, long life—anything you want. All you have to do is sell me your soul." The agent thinks for a minute and says, "What's the catch?"

Throughout 1969, Fred managed to get a television show produced called *Live from the Bitter End,* and it ran for most of the year. A minor technical error was the fact that the show wasn't live from the Bitter End. Fred had channel 9, the local station airing the show, build a studio set with tables and chairs and a red brick wall similar to the Bitter End. There are numerous videotaped copies of all those episodes floating around.

Anyone interested in seeing what the entertainment world of the sixties was really all about should try to find them. If anyone wants to see early performances of Neil Diamond the folksinger, Phil Ochs, Odetta, Janis Ian, the Simon Sisters, Ricky Nelson, the Mothers of Invention, Country Joe and the Fish, Woody Allen, Flip Wilson, David Steinberg, and hundreds more, that's where you'll find them. Actually, when the show first aired, Carly Simon and her sister, Lucy, were disbanding. Lucy wanted to concentrate on raising a family, so Carly got a part-time job as a secretary for the show. The guy who hired her said she was the worst secretary he had ever seen. Maybe because it was the sixties, the guy didn't fire her. He promoted her to assistant to the coordinator, and she wound up handling all the talent for the show. It was a year later when she made her solo debut at the club. Kris Kristofferson was the headliner.

Week by week the Bitter End grew as a rock club. I don't know whether it was luck or skill, but it seemed that by 1970 whoever was hot at that particular moment was booked into the club. We brought in the Lemon Pipers soon after their recording of "Green Tambourine" went gold. That was when I first met Neil Bogart from Buddha and Kama Sutra Records. After I helped Neil out with the Pipers, he sent all his subsequent acts to the Bitter End. We played Kensington Market, which was produced by Felix Pappalardi, McKendree Spring, Genya Ravan, and Ten Wheel Drive. We played Kenny Rankin when Kenny was first starting out at the club. Kenny called me up once and told me he couldn't make a particular gig. "But, Kenny, you played last night and everything was fine. What could have happened in twenty-four hours? Where are you?" "Paul, I haven't got a clue." Kenny only did that once, and I always gave an act a second chance.

I think what really established us as a rock club was the

Curtis Mayfield booking. Curtis came in and played a week for me in 1971, and it was a huge success. My friend Neil Bogart called and asked for the booking. I loved Neil and said, "Whatever week you want, just let me know." Neil and I booked a lot of great acts, and for some reason I never really questioned him about it. Singer-songwriter Jim Dawson, who was the opening act, couldn't believe it. In fact he was scared to death. "Do you mean I'm actually going to open for Curtis?" "Absolutely," I said. Agents and producers were calling the club nonstop. "Paul, can you save me a couple of seats for Curtis? I'll never ask you for another favor." "Absolutely," I said. Neil finally called me to make sure everything was set. I said, "Absolutely. By the way Neal, who the hell is Curtis?"

Now I knew who Curtis Mayfield was from the old days with the Impressions. It never occurred to me that my Curtis was that Curtis. Nobody like Curtis had ever played a club like the Bitter End before. Not only was he going to perform, but he was also going to record a live album. Jimi Hendrix had died the year before, and Curtis was able to use Jimi's mobile recording unit. On opening night the club was mobbed. It was filled with other artists, producers, agents, and reporters; there was hardly any room for the public.

Curtis had a quartet backing him up that included master Henry Gibson, as Curtis called him, on percussion. If Jim Dawson was nervous, so was Curtis. He had only recently broken with the Impressions, and he wasn't used to playing without his old partners. But the intimacy of the club and the fact that Bill Cosby and Diana Ross were in the audience eased the jitters. When Curtis and I spoke just before he died, he said, "The Bitter End definitely launched my career in a strong way because it showed my real value as a vocalist and an entertainer. It showed the real Curtis Mayfield."

The album is called *Curtis/Live!* and is still easily available. He did a lot of the old songs and some brand-new creations that wound up on the soundtrack for the movie *Superfly.* One of my favorite tunes was "If There's Hell Below, We're All Gonna Go." Whenever he came to the part about Nixon telling the people "Don't worry," the audiences would go crazy.

The Bitter End was one of Curtis's favorite places to play. "You're one with the people," he told me. And that's the way he liked it. The following year, as he promised, he came back and did another week at the club, and this was when *Superfly* was riding the charts. He could have filled Madison Square Garden, but he played my place instead. *Curtis/Live!* reached number twenty-one on the *Billboard* charts and stayed on the charts for almost forty weeks. God bless him.

Don McLean was a different matter. Despite our feuds, Hal Ray, who worked for William Morris, was still a good friend. One day he called and said, "Paul, please put in Don McLean." I put in Don McLean. This was before *American Pie,* when people were not bending over backwards to see him. Don had recorded a debut album called *Tapestry,* and he was dying to be heard.

Hal called me again and said, "Paul, please put in Don again." I said, "Hal, I love the kid, I love the album, but he doesn't do any business." "Please." I put him in three times, and he made no money for me. No business. Then one night I got another call to put Don in for a guest set. I said sure, and the place was mobbed. I didn't realize about the Chevy that fell off the levee. Don always traveled with his agent, Herb Gart, who was more than obnoxious. When Don saw the crowds out on the street, he and his agent came over and said, "Why don't you let them in for free?" I held my breath. "Don, I can't. The waitresses and the lighting and sound guys want to get paid. So do the opening acts. Remember how that was? How about you picking up the bill?" He didn't like that idea at all. I felt I made my point, but I wanted one other thing clear. I walked over to his manager and said, "You owe me one." Herb Gart said, "This is it." I said, "Fuck you. I played this guy when he couldn't get arrested. You owe me a week." He started making demands, he had a lawyer call me. Don never played for me again. When I first met Andy Warhol, we shook hands and I said, "Can I have a whole hour?" making a joke on his "fifteen minutes of fame" line. A lot of people are very famous for a brief moment, but real fame is the kind that spreads out and grows upward. Real fame involves class. Don McLean is out there somewhere, and as far as I'm concerned, he still owes me one more show.

After Curtis came and recorded his live album, we began booking soul acts and Motown groups, reggae bands, and rhythm and blues artists. Donny Hathaway recorded a live album; Billy Paul, Taj Mahal, Johnny Nash, the Persuasions, and Billy Preston all played the club. Stevie Wonder was the most exciting act we ever had in the Bitter End. Stevie came in with a thirteen-piece band and three girl singers and did fourteen shows during the week they appeared. Every show was sold out. The stage was so crowded it almost defied physics. Jerry Jeff Walker walked in during a set and couldn't believe the place. It was a madhouse. I thought the cops were going to come and close us down. People were dancing in the aisles. Jerry grabbed somebody's Coke, poured something from a flask into it, and started dancing in the aisles with everybody else. He just kept dancing and yelling "Holy shit! Holy shit!" I remember the backup singers came up to me and said, "Please talk him into coming back . . . please."

I should say right now that jazz was also holding on to an audience during the sixties and seventies much more than it is these days. If you were into rock, it was almost part of the program to allow jazz to enter your world at least a little bit. Jazz was respected, and people always came to the shows. But you could tell who was really into jazz and who wasn't. If you really wanted to see jazz, you went to a jazz club. But jazz musicians wanted the work desperately. They wanted to try to tap into the rock audience, who they perceived as being open-minded. Once when I had Larry Coryell booked for a week, I needed an opening act. Larry was very jazzy, a purist, and I knew only purists would dig him. I called up Chick Corea and said, "Chick, I don't have any money in the budget but I have an opening." He said, "I'll take it." Chick had recently left Miles Davis and was starting his own band called Return to Forever. It became a fusion band but at the time had a real groovy Latin flavor to it. You have no idea what that show did for Chick. Hardly anyone mentioned poor Larry, but Chick got rave reviews. It turned his career around 180 degrees.

One of my favorite performers was Bette Midler. Irvin Arthur took me to see her when she was doing spots at Upstairs at the Downstairs, which was a somewhat chichi nightclub in midtown. Irvin thought she'd be great at the Bitter End. I loved her act but wasn't sure how she would fit into the club, which was most definitely downtown. What killed me was that Bette was dying to play the club. I think she was going out with Buzzy Linhart's drummer at the time. She used one of Buzz's songs, "Friends," as her theme song.

When I booked Bette, the phone almost rang off the hook. Neil Bogart, who was trying to sign her to Buddha, was absolutely fulsome. "Paul, you've got Bette. You've got to give me the opening act." I did, which turned out to be a band called Stories. But Neil didn't stop there. "Paul, I want to redo your dressing room." He had painters come in, he put new rugs on the floor, which was odd because there were never any old rugs. He sent in furniture that included chairs from the film *A Clockwork Orange*. The funky back room actually looked pretty upscale for once.

A couple of days before the show I got a call from somebody representing Bette. It was a sheepish voice. "Paul, you have to do me a favor. You have to put a sign outside that reads 'Music arranged and conducted by Barry Manilow.'" "Who the fuck is Barry Manilow?" "Please, Paul." "What do you think this is, Carnegie Hall?" "Paul, pretty please." So I put out the sign. On opening night a lot of gay fans who had been following Bette since the old days at the Continental Baths came swishing into the Bitter End. One guy looked around, took out a handkerchief, dusted off his seat, and then turned to his partner and said, "What a dump!"

Every show was sold out. *Newsweek* magazine did a review of the show, and Bette was really being talked about. Probably the most significant part of the engagement, however, was that Aaron Russo and his wife were at the show. Aaron was, and is, a big Hollywood producer. He was the first producer to ask for and get a million bucks. His movies, like *Trading Places,* have received six Academy Awards to date. It took a few more months, but he finally talked Bette into letting him represent her. He would eventually go on to make *The Rose,* starring Bette Midler. My favorite Aaron Russo line is that IRS stands for "It really sucks."

Bette went on to sign with Ahmet Ertegun and Atlantic Records. But the kicker came after the Bitter End appearance when she and Barry rented out Carnegie Hall, which was an incredible gamble. By the night of the show in June of 1972 they had sold the place out. As I walked through the doors to attend the performance, I saw a huge poster that read "Bette Midler" and below it, "Musical Director: Barry Manilow." I couldn't help thinking, "The world is upside down. Now Carnegie Hall is copying me." Bette and I stayed in touch for years. She still came down to the club whenever she could, and later, when her fame became astronomical, she always made sure there were passes for me to her concerts. She is a great friend.

In an odd way Peter Allen had a lot in common with Bette Midler. By the time I met Peter, he was already separated from Liza Minnelli. It was an upsetting breakup for a lot of reasons, not the least of which was the fact that Judy Garland had discovered him in Australia and brought him back to America. Peter came into the club a couple of years before Bette. He was trying to find himself. I used to hang out at his apartment. We both knew that he was meant for the swankier clubs, but he appreciated the work. Peter was on a very fast track, and not just sex and stimulants. He was relentlessly trying to create an image. His songs were nice and had a real pop feel. He knew how to write a hit. But, like Bette, he was very much into putting on a show. He had no interest in sitting moodily behind the piano. At the end of 1972, after Bette finished her gig at the club, Peter was opening for her at the Troubadour in Los Angeles.

When Dion played the club, he also recorded a live album. Dion was trying to revitalize his career. His hits had come in the early sixties, and it seemed like the music business was leaving him behind. I know he had a lot of personal problems. I love Dion because he decided the fastest way back to the top was to write a new hit, and he did. "Abraham, Martin, and John" was one of those rare records. It's a song that could have been seen as sentimental or even sacrilegious, but when Dion sang it, everyone knew it came from the heart. It was a gas watching the younger kids listen to "Abraham, Martin, and John," which is what they paid to hear, and then sit there stunned listening to

"Run-Around Sue" and "The Wanderer." "Oh my God," they would say. "It's the same guy."

To a lot of people it must seem that the Bitter End either gets people on the way up or on the way down or trying to make a comeback. To a certain extent that's true. Things happen so fast in the music business that it's impossible to always know what the public will go for. But there were wonderful moments when all the stars were in perfect alignment. I listened to an Andy Gibb album for about five minutes and immediately called up his agent. I wanted this act. The agent was surprised, because no one else seemed to be interested. We booked a date about a month in advance, and by that weekend Andy's song "I Just Want to Be Your Everything" was in the top ten and rising. The agent tried to cancel the gig, and Andy wouldn't hear of it. "Paul Colby believed in me before anybody." He played the club when he probably could have filled the Garden. I know this because a week later he filled the Nassau Coliseum out on Long Island. He was a tender and sensitive guy. I think life and the business just became too much for him. I know Andy overdosed on drugs, but it wasn't the kind of crazy excess that killed Jimi Hendrix and Janis Joplin, who used to come to the club often as a patron. Andy died of a broken heart.

I pulled the same kind of coup with America and booked them well in advance of any popularity. It didn't take a genius to realize that "A Horse with No Name" was going to be a hit. The week of America's performance they had the number-one record in the country. Those three guys were so nervous they were shaking. The place was packed and there were lines around the block. The publicity was wild. CBS had announced the gig as a breaking news story. The entire top floor of Warner Brothers was in the audience. These kids were the golden boys, and I had them for a week. The funny thing was that they were the opening act. I figured the song would be big but not that big. Hundreds of people wanted to see these guys, and I could only put them on for about twenty minutes. America didn't mind because they really weren't that seasoned yet and they didn't have a lot of material. But they sang like angels. One night, in between sets, I saw one of them out on Bleecker Street with a real glum look on his face. I thought he was upset about the performance or the club, but, no, he was too young to get served alcohol in the bar next door. He didn't have any proof.

Bruce Springsteen was a nice memory. Everybody talks about Bruce as the New Jersey boy. He was born there, and he played in little clubs near the Jersey shore for years. But he never got discovered until he came to Greenwich Village. He used to do solo sets up at Max's Kansas City. Everybody in the industry knew him because he used to open for Dave Van Ronk and Odetta. Somebody would always bring up his name. He even auditioned for John Hammond's band across the street from us. David Blue picked him up one night and brought him down to the club to hear Jackson Browne. They hung out at the club all night.

When Billy Joel came back to New York after a stint in California playing piano in a small bar, he had written most of the material for "Piano Man." People think it was that experience that gave him the inspiration for the song, but it's not so. Billy actually wrote "Piano Man" after seeing Bob Dylan at the Bitter End. He couldn't remember the song, but Dylan was at the piano. Dylan also had his harmonica rack around his neck, and at first Billy wasn't sure what the thing was for. He thought there was something wrong with Dylan's teeth. People are always telling stories like that. Leo Kottke taught himself the guitar by listening to Pete Seeger's live album called *The Bitter and the Sweet*. The first time he ever heard a twelve-string guitar was on that album. Leo is one of the greatest twelve-string practitioners around.

The transition worked. By 1975 we were one of the best rock venues in the country. We either booked or were destined to book the best names in rock. Michael Franks, Delaney Bramlett, Brian Auger, Dr. John, Luther Allison, Tori Amos, Little Feat, Stephen Bishop, Sarah McLachlan, G Love and Special Sauce. As of 2002, the Bitter End is now considered the oldest rock club in the country.

George Thorogood said that there were very few good places to play anymore, but he listed the Bitter End as one of the best. New faces like Ricky Byrd, who toured with Joan Jett and the Blackhearts, began his solo career at the club. At present we play and help develop new bands like Burlap to Cashmere and Rusted Root. In that respect the Bitter End still holds with tradition. It seems like we either hold on to tradition or break tradition and start a new tradition. Who cares? It's a tradition.

11

N~O~ E~ND IN~ S~IGHT~

I have my faults, but changing my tune is not one of them.
　　　　　　　　　　—Samuel Beckett, *The Unnamable*

THERE'S AN OLD JOKE ABOUT A GUY who cleans up after the elephants in the circus. One day, watching him shovel, his buddy hears him cursing like crazy. "Hey," his friend says, "if you don't like it, why don't you quit?" The guy replies, "What, and give up show business?"

Well, I'm one of the luckiest guys in the world. In July 2001, the Bitter End celebrated its fortieth anniversary and I celebrated sixty years in show business. I must admit that sometimes I felt like the guy shoveling the shit. I must admit that every once in a while, things do go wrong. Like the time the heating system went haywire during a Christmas-week show. I forgot to buy an extra space heater for the dressing room, and Janis Ian, who was headlining, caught a sore throat and had to cancel some shows. Odetta wanted to kill me, but it was just one of those times when you can only say, "I'm sorry." Or more recently when Hunter Payne played the club. There was a drunk in the first row who was heckling Hunter. After repeated attempts to quiet him down, we finally had to throw the guy out. We solved the heckling problem, but it wasn't the kind of milieu that Hunter would have liked for his quiet and soulful songs. But the Bitter End is not a second or third take. It's as alive as it gets. For me, there is no other way to live life.

The day the Bitter End was given landmark status by the city of New York, July 23, 1992, I began reflecting on all the history I've been a part of and that I've been allowed to participate in. To read my name mentioned with Bob Dylan, Peter, Paul and Mary, Billy Crystal, George Carlin, Curtis Mayfield, and others is still a thrill for me. And even if I'm not mentioned personally, the Bitter End is referenced in thousands of books and articles. The Bitter End has evolved into a kind of shrine that fans and artists are still eager to make pilgrimages to. And it's still a lighthouse for anyone crazy enough to go out on the rough seas of the entertainment world. It's still the center of the universe. Let me reflect.

I mentioned thousands of books and articles. One of the most interesting literary references came from novelist Jack Engelhard, author of *Indecent Proposal*. His follow-up book, published in 1998, was called *The Days of the Bitter End*. It tells the story of a Vaughn Meader character, a star comedian who does imitations of JFK. It follows him during the days just after Kennedy gets shot, and his career takes a predictable nosedive. The Bitter End and numerous historical personalities are all part of the landscape. Even Fred Weintraub is a character. Jack Engelhard knows exactly what he's talking about because back in the early sixties Jack was a doorman at the club. We held the release party at the club, and Jack signed copies of his book. It's available only on the Internet. It was one of the first examples of on-line publications.

It's remarkable, yet only fitting, that the Bitter End is still deeply connected to literature and the literary scene. Besides Rod McKuen and Muhammad Ali, the club has always been home to the best of the beat poets like Allen Ginsberg. Every year now the club plays host to a celebration of the life of Jack Kerouac. We try to hold it in the spring around Earth Day. Of course, iconoclastic as always, we call it Earth Night. For the 2000 festival we had David Amram, Vic Juris, Victor Venegas, Paul Krassner, Levi Asher, Brian Hassett, Bob Wiseman, and Neal Cassady's kid John performing, reading, and generally making wonderful mayhem. We produced the show in conjunction with VH1's *Save the Music,* which collects used instruments and pumps them back into local public school music programs. If you donated an instrument, you got in for free.

We hold regular events like the Literary Kicks Summer Poetry Happening. I like to think of it as keeping the beat alive. There are often tom-tom processions and American Indian blessings. David Amram playing five horns and flutes at once. Bob Wiseman playing prepared piano à la John Cage. Brian Hassett running like mad, reading his poetry, and introducing everybody, including the Mighty Manatees Medicine Show. After we held this event, my manager, Paul Rizzo, invited everybody and anybody back to do it again. Who knows, maybe it will be a new tradition.

The traditions and the connections tumble through my memory and through the memories of millions of others who performed or came to see and hear shows over the past forty years.

Jim Rooney is a musician and coauthor, with Eric Von Schmidt, of *Baby Let Me Follow You Down,* a retrospective of the Cambridge, Massachusetts, music scene. He tells a great story of running into Dylan in the very early sixties at the Dugout, the old shot-and-beer place next to the Bitter End. As they talked, Dylan suggested they go over to the club and play. It was Tuesday night and there was a hoot. Jim said he was just there and the Bitter End was mobbed. Dylan didn't care. The two went inside the club and asked Theo Bikel if they could go on. Bikel was the emcee that night, and he said no, they were booked solid. Dylan didn't care about that either. He stood off in the corner near the funky back room, took out his guitar, and began to play and sing. Pretty soon they had a crowd around them.

But one of my favorite and oddest stories, and a perfect example of how the Bitter End touches people's lives, involves the great writer for the *Greenwich Village Gazette,* Tony Bartoli. Tony first became connected to the Bitter End when he played the hoots back in the old days with a kind of jug band called the Sanjac of Novipazar. Tony was the drummer and he loved playing, but the band eventually broke up. Tony then found himself involved in Wavy Gravy's commune, the Hog Farm. The Hog Farm has a firm place in the sixties peace-and-love mythology, but Tony was ready to pull up stakes. He decided to say farewell and stopped by a Greenwich Village loft where some Hog Farm members were hanging out when Wavy Gravy's lover, a girl named Bonnie Jean, asked if Tony would take her to the Bitter End. He was surprised but pleased, and they left for the club. It was a warm and pleasant summer night.

That evening the club had Spider John Koerner and Willie Murphy on the bill. Bonnie then told Tony that she had been born and raised in Minnesota and used to hang out at a bar where John Koerner used to play and where Dylan hung out, that she actually went out with Dylan, and that he had written a song about her. It was the famous and beautiful "Girl from the North Country." After the set Tony and Bonnie Jean went to the funky back room, and John Koerner almost fell off his stool. "Oh my God. How have you been? Do you see Bob anymore?" Yes, it was all true. And Tony tells it with a hint of sadness, like the story of a beautiful dream and the dreamer realizing that he must soon wake up. Wavy Gravy, Bob Dylan, Spider John, and the Bitter End. It's nice to remember.

I've been pleased to discover over the years that other artists besides the performing kind got a boost up in their careers from hanging out at the Bitter End. Photographer Mark Roth had an exhibit of his work at our restaurant, the Tin Angel, right above the club. It was at that show that he first met Joni Mitchell, and they began working together. His work includes album covers he had done for Bitter End acts like Steve Gillette. His cover for "Sunday Will Never Be the Same" by Spanky and Our Gang was the first foldout album cover for a single record in the history of rock and roll. After that cover design came out, record companies would use the foldout concept as a statement that they were really behind that particular artist. That they were willing to spend the extra money to create a booklike presentation meant that whoever the particular artist was, he or she or they had truly arrived. Mark went on to do the great album covers and publicity shots for Joni Mitchell. He is one of the most respected photographers in the business.

Harry Gittes was a jazz musician and a copywriter in New York back in the early sixties. In order to supplement his income, he used to come down to the Bitter End and shoot the new up-and-coming acts. Harry did publicity work and album covers for Woody Allen, Jim, Jake and Joan, Bill Cosby, Cass Elliot, and even Professor Irwin Cory. He became friends with Roy Silver, and Roy took Harry out to Hollywood, where he eventually became a film producer. Harry Gittes produced *Little Nikita* with River Phoenix and *Goin' South,* which was Bitter End alumnus John Belushi's first movie. Harry's friend Jack Nicholson starred in and directed it. When Jack Nicholson did *Chinatown,* he had his character, Jake, named after Harry.

One of the great *Billboard* photographers, Chuck Pulin, has shot more pictures at the Bitter End than anyplace else. Chuck is also a formidable writer and occasionally supplements his pictures with great articles for the top publications. One of our favorite bartenders, Danny Shanahan, is now a first-rate cartoonist whose work is not only anthologized but still appears regularly in the *New Yorker* magazine.

Probably the most famous photographer to work the Village was Fred McDarrah. His photographs are world famous. One of my two favorites is the shot he did of Bobby Kennedy in 1967 visiting a tenement slum in L.A. He's standing in front of a gray wall, and tilted above his head is a portrait of a crucified Christ almost looking down on him. The other is the photograph of Cassius Clay walking to his poetry reading at the Bitter End in 1963. I think a signed copy goes for seventeen hundred dollars.

We finally got our due mention in film when NBC ran their miniseries *The Sixties* in the beginning of 1999. There's a scene where the two main characters are in the Village talking to each other in front of the Bitter End. Just as they begin to depart, a curly-haired guy dressed in black and carrying a guitar case comes out of the club. The doorman says, "Good night, Bob," as the actor gives a Dylanish wave of his hand. Oh well. *The Sixties* wasn't *Gone with the Wind,* but they did get a great shot of the sign.

It was only natural that they put us in the movie. People have often told me that whenever they walk into the Bitter End, it's like entering a time machine. Not only because of the way the club looks, the brick wall, the old posters, but something else. A feeling. I think that's why people keep coming back.

When the U.S. Postal Service decided to honor the Woodstock festival, they held the first-day-of-issue ceremony at the club. It was actually part of a series called Celebrating the Century. People all over the country voted for events worth memorializing on a stamp, and Woodstock was one of them. Right up there with the Beatles and Neil Armstrong walking on the moon. It was particularly poignant for all of us at the club because of the close kinship we had with so many of the original performers. And of course it was Fred Weintraub who helped bring the event to the big screen.

Besides all the post office brass, Mike Lang, Joel Rosenman, and John Roberts were there. These were the guys who created the Woodstock festival. Mickey Hart from the Grateful Dead, one of the original performers, stopped by too. The summer of 1969 seemed long ago and far away. Most of the postal officials in attendance weren't even born then. Robert Kennedy Jr. dropped in. When I introduced myself, Kennedy said, "I've been to your club before." I said, "That's nice. Did you spend a lot of money?" He didn't say, but he autographed my stamp.

When A&E wanted to do a biography of George Carlin, they came down to the club, shot some footage, and interviewed me. George Carlin's office recommended it to CBS, who did the production work. And when Jon Stewart was having a feature TV exposé done on him after he became a star, they asked him at what spots he would like to be interviewed. He said the Bitter End. "If it wasn't for the Bitter End, I wouldn't be here today." I already told the story of Jon and Wendy Wall. When Jon came in for the shoot, we made sure Wendy stopped by. They had a very emotional meeting. It's moments like that that make it a good career.

I always get a kick out of celebrities who stop by to visit or see a show. I always make sure they're not bothered, and the best way to do that is to sit with them. One of my favorite nights was

spent with the actor Albert Finney. He called me over to thank
me for the hospitality, and I had a drink with him. I told him that
one of my favorite movies was *Two for the Road* with him and
Audrey Hepburn. In the film, while trying to work out marital
problems, they drive all over Europe in a white Mercedes 230SL.
I said, "Albert, I was so impressed with your performance and
that car that I went out and bought one. I got my car from *Two
for the Road*." "Yes," said Finney with wry smile, "you may have
gotten the car, but did you get Audrey Hepburn?"

Occasionally the celebrity was another club owner or
ex–club owner like Albert Grossman or Earl Pionke. Earl had a
club in Chicago called Earl of Old Town. Tons of people played
there. John Prine played there before he came to New York and
got signed at the Bitter End. Earl once flew in from Chicago with
five other people to hear Bonnie Koloc play the club. The party
dropped half a grand and Earl picked up the whole tab.

More recently the Bitter End hosted a party for Ramblin'
Jack Elliott. Jack's daughter Aiyana made a very good documentary about her dad called *The Ballad of Ramblin' Jack*. Anybody interested in Woody Guthrie and Bob Dylan and the link
that connects them must see it. The link is Jack. *Vanity Fair* covered the party and did a feature story on Jack, Aiyana, and the
film. They sent Annie Leibovitz down to do the photography.
That's how I got the picture for the frontispiece of this book.
Odetta stopped by to say hello. Jack had me laughing when he
said, "I'm so sick of this routine. It's draining my vitality." Anybody else in the world would be basking in the notoriety and
renewed interest that a feature-length documentary could bring,
but not Jack. That's why I always liked Jack. He didn't give a
curse. He seemed more interested in being a missing link. But
that's Jack, always taking the road not taken.

People are always sending me vignettes about the club, like

when my niece Helen Colby sent me actor Ethan Hawke's first novel. It was called *The Hottest State,* and on page one Hawke introduces the two main characters meeting for the first time at the Bitter End. There's a long, involved pickup scene that ends with the soon-to-be-lovers walking home, early in morning, through Washington Square Park.

The great jazz critic Fred Bouchard attended one of the nights we had Gil Evans and his orchestra. He was sitting next to Sy Johnson, and after the show and the talk with Sy he wrote an article and sent it in to *Downbeat* magazine without an introduction as to who he was. He happened to be teaching in Massachusetts, and they called him up and asked him if he wanted to be their Boston correspondent.

The songwriter George Gerdes tells a story of seeing Tim Hardin at the Bitter End. In the middle of the show Tim stood his guitar straight up by balancing it on the strap peg. Imagine balancing something bulky on the edge of a dime. But there it is, standing vertically. No strings. Tim studied this for a minute and then with outstretched hands said, "Suspense. The key to the act is—suspense." Then he went over to the piano and played "Hang On to a Dream." He walked back and picked up the guitar, and it fell into hands like it had been hypnotized.

It's a mistake to live in the past, but it's difficult to turn aside all the great moments that have occurred at the club and in the Village. One thing you can always do is make the past relevant to the present, and that's what Art D'Lugoff and I are doing with the help of Odetta, Judy Collins, Pete Seeger, and others. Art and I are helping to create the Greenwich Village Folk Music Museum. The history of folk music and all the performers who made folk music important will be celebrated. There will be photography, artwork, memorabilia, live performances on film, a literary and musical library, and a concert stage.

We held our first fund-raiser at the great hall at Cooper Union on June 14, 2000. The indefatigable Oscar Brand was the moderator. Bethany Yarrow opened the show, followed by Odetta, Pete Seeger, John Coen from the New Lost City Ramblers, Josh White Jr., John Sebastian, John Hammond Jr., David Amram, and Judy Collins. Everybody got up and sang three or four songs. It reminded me of hoot night at the Bitter End. The concert ran late. We ended the show with everyone singing onstage for the grand finale. We all sang "We Shall Build a Folk Museum" to the tune of "We Shall Overcome." Everybody had a great time, and we raised a lot of money. With the help of producer Tommy Senif we created a website (www.folkmusicmuseum.com), had the whole show filmed for television, and recorded a CD. Of course the CD will be out on Bitter End Records.

Bitter End Records is an idea I wanted to pursue for a long time, like writing a book. With the invaluable assistance of Tom Senif, we released our first CD, an album by Bitter End regular Chris Glen, in the fall of 2000. Having artists who played the Bitter End cut records or CDs is not a new phenomenon, but recording them on Bitter End Records is. Probably the best indication of what the club is like now is to pick up a copy of *Tommy James and the Shondells: Live at the Bitter End*. Tommy recorded his greatest hits at the club in 1998 and brought a film crew with him. The sound is great, the show is great, and it's available on CD, videotape, and DVD. Talk about keeping up with the times.

Of course it's all very gratifying to have Rhino Records list the Bitter End as the most popular Greenwich Village hangout. Or to see that the Everly Brothers include us as one of their most successful venues along with the Paramount Theatre, the Hollywood Bowl, the Latin Quarter, and Caesar's Palace. Or to be part of a course taught at NYU on the early days of folk music and the club scene. Now that's being a part of history. Actually, Fred

Weintraub taught a course on the Bitter End at Berkeley years ago after he moved to California.

People still try to typecast us. The Bitter End is mentioned in thousands of guidebooks from all over the world, and they always list us as "old folk club" or "historic folk club." Then they usually go on to tell the reader that we really don't play folk music anymore. Last year we sponsored the ASCAP (American Society of Composers, Authors, and Publishers) New York Songwriters Circle Showcase. We have hosted Ozzy Osbourne tribute concerts. We regularly play Burlap to Cashmere, a contemporary Christian act, to packed houses, as well as the Moshar Band, a hot Jewish folk rock ensemble. If we ever lose our focus, we bring in Paul Krassner. Paul does a stand-up comedy routine these days, but most of you will likely know him as the founder and still editor of the *Realist*. The *Realist* was founded in the fifties. Joseph Heller told Paul he writes *Catch-22* with each issue. Paul made history when he wrote in the *Realist* that there might be evidence to prove LBJ had committed necrophilia on Air Force One after the assassination by fucking JFK in the bullet hole. Many people found the story perfectly believable. Does that sound to you like a historic folk club?

One of the most satisfying experiences is seeing the kids of performers play the club. Being the child of a star is always a little rough, especially if the kid wants to follow in the parent's footsteps. There is often a programmed sense of expectation and disappointment in the mind of the audience, especially when the kids do something stylistically different from their folks. All I know is the apple doesn't fall too far from the tree. Over the years we have played Jen Chapin, Harry's daughter; Sarah Lee and Abe Guthrie, two of Arlo's kids; Jim Croce's son A. J.; Diana Ross's stepdaughter Leona Naess; Jenni Muldaur, the daughter of Maria and Geoffrey; Pete Seeger's grandson Tao Rodriguez;

Paul Simon's son Harper; Leonard Cohen's son Adam; Stevie Stills's son Chris; Lucy Simon's daughter Julia; Peter Yarrow's daughter Bethany; Berry Oakley, whose dad, Raymond Berry Oakley, was the original bassist for the Allman Brothers; Cassie Berns, the daughter of my good friend Bert; and Sally Taylor, the daughter of Carly Simon and James Taylor. When James Taylor was being interviewed by Charlie Rose for *Sixty Minutes II*, they did most of the shooting at the Bitter End. When James walked in the door, we hugged, and then I showed him a picture of his daughter and me just after her performance. Sally had made her debut just weeks before, on the same stage where her father had performed thirty years earlier.

A friend sent me an excerpt from an etymological book by Webb Garrison called *Why You Say It*. One question was, "Why is pursuing something to the ultimate called going to the 'bitter end'?" The answer started out by saying, "There's a famous café in New York City called The Bitter End where many Beatnik poets read from their works in the 1950's and early 60's. But if any establishment would call itself the Bitter End and be true to the expression's origin, you would find it on the waterfront because the phrase comes from the age of sailing ships." Then the book went on to tell about a wooden log called a bitt that held the anchor at some point. If you had to drop anchor in deep sea, the bitt was used as a warning marker. If you dropped anchor but hadn't hit bottom by the time you got to the bitt it was, well, the bitter end.

I like that image. A lot of people dropped anchor in this place, and some of them didn't survive. But for most it was a good temporary home. There was a girl named Carol Hall from Abilene, Texas. She was in and out of the music business for years but dropped out in the sixties to raise a family. The marriage didn't work out, but she got a gig at the Bitter End working with Kris Kristofferson. She eventually wound up writing the words and music for *The Best Little Whorehouse in Texas*. Or when Phoebe Snow got discovered at the club and within a year won the Grammy award.

I could tell you a thousand stories like this, but my favorite memories are special images. Lucy and Carly Simon, still in school, taking the train back and forth from Connecticut to New York every weekend to play the club. Or the great story of Neil Diamond and the *Tonight Show* when Fred, who was managing Neil, had the NBC talent scouts come down to the club to hear him. Neil, who wanted to show how versatile he was, picked "If I Ruled the World" to sing. He completely screwed up the performance and didn't get on the *Tonight Show* until years later. The first time I heard Shawn Colvin sing. Moments that make you laugh, cause you to admire, and make you pause in wonder.

People are always asking me what the Bitter End means to me. Whether I'm being interviewed for *Billboard* magazine or Japanese television, I usually say something deflective or self-deprecating. For the record, one last story sums up my club pretty accurately. In 1997 I was given the Platinum Record Award for Lifetime Achievement. I was one of a handful of people including deejay Scott Muni, my friend and concert promoter Sid Bernstein, songwriter George David Weiss, and producer Phil Ramone. Roger Daltrey and Joan Jett came by to give Scott his award. Richie Havens was my presenter. When Phil Ramone accepted his award, he graciously acknowledged every other recipient. He thanked Sid for bringing the Beatles to America. He thanked George Weiss for writing "What A Wonderful World" for Louis Armstrong. He thanked Scott for playing the records and standing behind the artists. And then he paused and said, "You know, I was in the studio the other day with Billy Joel. We were recording a new album. Billy suddenly got introspective and said, 'Phil, can you believe where we are? It's amazing. What if we woke up and it were all taken away from us?' I said, 'Billy, not to worry. I'll grab my saxophone and the two of us will go down and see Paul. No matter what happens, we can always get a gig at the Bitter End.'"

We're still at 147 Bleecker Street in the heart of Greenwich Village. You should stop down. You never know who might be hanging out on any given night. Stop down even if it's just to say hello. I'll be there. I'll be there till the bitter end.

INDEX

Index

OTHER COOPER SQUARE PRESS TITLES OF INTEREST

ANY OLD WAY YOU CHOOSE IT
ROCK AND OTHER POP MUSIC, 1967–1973
Expanded Edition
Robert Christgau
360 pp.
0-8154-1041-7
$16.95

THE ART PEPPER COMPANION
WRITINGS ON A JAZZ ORIGINAL
Edited by Todd Selbert
300 pp., 4 color photos, 16 b/w photos
0-8154-1067-0
$30.00 cloth

BACKSTAGE PASSES
LIFE ON THE WILD SIDE WITH
DAVID BOWIE
Angela Bowie with Patrick Carr
368 pp., 36 b/w photos
0-8154-1001-8
$17.95

BEHIND BLUE EYES
THE LIFE OF PETE TOWNSHEND
with new afterword
Geoffrey Giuliano
376 pp., 17 b/w photos
0-8154-1070-0
$17.95

THE BLUES
IN IMAGES AND INTERVIEWS
Robert Neff and Anthony Connor
152 pp., 84 b/w photos
0-8154-1003-4
$17.95

CHER
IF YOU BELIEVE
Mark Bego
Foreword by Mary Wilson
464 pp., 50 b/w photos
0-8154-1153-7
$27.95 cloth

COLONEL TOM PARKER
THE CURIOUS LIFE OF ELVIS PRESLEY'S
ECCENTRIC MANAGER
James L. Dickerson
310 pp., 35 b/w photos
0-8154-1088-3
$27.95 cloth

DEPECHE MODE
A BIOGRAPHY
Steve Malins
280 pp., 24 b/w photos
0-8154-1142-1
$17.95

DESPERADOS
THE ROOTS OF COUNTRY ROCK
John Einarson
304 pp., 31 b/w photos
0-8154-1065-4
$19.95

DID THEY MENTION THE MUSIC?
THE AUTOBIOGRAPHY OF HENRY MANCINI
Updated Edition
Henry Mancini with Gene Lees
312 pp., 44 b/w photos
0-8154-1175-8
$18.95

DREAMGIRL AND SUPREME FAITH
MY LIFE AS A SUPREME
Updated Edition
Mary Wilson
732 pp., 150 b/w photos, 15 color photos
0-8154-1000-X
$19.95

FAITHFULL
AN AUTOBIOGRAPHY
Marianne Faithfull with David Dalton
320 pp., 32 b/w photos
0-8154-1046-8
$16.95

FREAKSHOW
MISADVENTURES IN THE COUNTERCULTURE,
1959–1971
Albert Goldman
416 pp.
0-8154-1169-3
$17.95

GO WHERE YOU WANNA GO
THE ORAL HISTORY OF THE MAMAS AND
THE PAPAS
Matthew Greenwald
Introduction by Andrew Loog Oldham
304 pp., 44 b/w photos
0-8154-1204-5
$25.95 cloth

GOIN' BACK TO MEMPHIS
A CENTURY OF BLUES, ROCK 'N' ROLL,
AND GLORIOUS SOUL
James Dickerson
284 pp., 58 b/w photos
0-8154-1049-2
$16.95

**HARMONICAS, HARPS, AND HEAVY
BREATHERS**
THE EVOLUTION OF THE PEOPLE'S
INSTRUMENT
Updated Edition
Kim Field
392 pp., 44 b/w photos
0-8154-1020-4
$18.95

HE'S A REBEL
PHIL SPECTOR—ROCK AND ROLL'S
LEGENDARY PRODUCER
Mark Ribowsky
368 pp., 35 b/w photos
0-8154-1044-1
$18.95

JOHN CAGE: WRITER
SELECTED TEXTS
Edited and introduced by Richard
Kostelanetz
304 pp., 15 illustrations, facsimiles, and
reproductions
0-1854-1034-4
$17.95

JUST FOR A THRILL
LIL HARDIN ARMSTRONG, FIRST LADY
OF JAZZ
James L. Dickerson
350 pp., 15 b/w photos
0-8154-1195-2
$26.95 cloth

LENNON IN AMERICA
1971–1980, BASED IN PART ON THE LOST
LENNON DIARIES
Geoffrey Giuliano
320 pp., 68 b/w photos
0-8154-1157-X
$17.95

LIVING WITH THE DEAD
TWENTY YEARS ON THE BUS WITH GARCIA
AND THE GRATEFUL DEAD
Rock Scully with David Dalton
408 pp., 31 b/w photos
0-8154-1163-4
$17.95

LOUIS' CHILDREN
AMERICAN JAZZ SINGERS
Updated Edition
Leslie Gourse
384 pp.
0-8154-1114-6
$18.95

MADONNA
BLONDE AMBITION
Updated Edition
Mark Bego
368 pp., 57 b/w photos
0-8154-1051-4
$18.95

MICK JAGGER
PRIMITIVE COOL
Updated Edition
Chris Sandford
352 pp., 56 b/w photos
0-8154-1002-6
$16.95

OSCAR PETERSON
THE WILL TO SWING
Updated Edition
Gene Lees
328 pp., 15 b/w photos
0-8154-1021-2
$18.95

REMINISCING WITH NOBLE SISSLE AND EUBIE BLAKE
Robert Kimball and William Bolcom
256 pp., 244 b/w photos
0-8154-1045-X
$24.95

ROCK 100
THE GREATEST STARS OF ROCK'S GOLDEN AGE
with a new introduction
David Dalton and Lenny Kaye
288 pp., 195 b/w photos
0-8154-1017-4
$19.95

ROCK SHE WROTE
WOMEN WRITE ABOUT ROCK, POP, AND RAP
Edited by Evelyn McDonnell and Ann Powers
496 pp.
0-8154-1018-2
$16.95

SUMMER OF LOVE
THE INSIDE STORY OF LSD, ROCK & ROLL, FREE LOVE AND HIGH TIMES IN THE WILD WEST
Joel Selvin
392 pp., 23 b/w photos
0-8154-1019-0
$16.95

SWING UNDER THE NAZIS
JAZZ AS A METAPHOR FOR FREEDOM
with a new preface
Mike Zwerin
232 pp., 45 b/w photos
0-8154-1075-1
$17.95

TEMPTATIONS
Updated Edition
Otis Williams with Patricia Romanowski
288 pp., 57 b/w photos
$17.95
0-8154-1218-5

TURNED ON
A BIOGRAPHY OF HENRY ROLLINS
James Parker
280 pp., 10 b/w photos
0-8154-1050-6
$17.95

UNFORGETTABLE
THE LIFE AND MYSTIQUE OF NAT KING COLE
Leslie Gourse
352 pp., 32 b/w illustrations
0-8154-1082-4
$17.95

WAITING FOR DIZZY
FOURTEEN JAZZ PORTRAITS
Gene Lees
Foreword by Terry Teachout
272 pp.
0-8154-1037-9
$17.95

WESTSIDE
THE COAST-TO-COAST EXPLOSION OF HIP HOP
William Shaw
334 pp.
0-8154-1196-0
$16.95

WILLIE
AN AUTOBIOGRAPHY
Willie Nelson and Bud Shrake
368 pp., 72 b/w photos
0-8154-1080-8
$18.95

Available at bookstores; or call 1-800-462-6420

COOPER SQUARE PRESS
200 Park Avenue South
Suite 1109
New York, NY 10003